MW00794946

Don't Spit on My Corner

Miguel Durán

Arte Publico Press
Houston
Texas
1992

This volume is made possible through a grant from the National Endowment for the Arts, a federal agency.

Arte Publico Press
University of Houston
Houston, Texas 77204-2090

Cover design by Mark Piñón

Don't Spit on My Corner / Miguel Durán
          p.   cm.
    ISBN 1-55885-042-2
    I. Title.
PS3554.U64D6 1992
813'.54–dc20   91-29104
                                                          CIP

The paper used in this publication meets the requirements of the American National Standard for Permanence of Paper for Printed Library Materials Z39.48-1984. ∞

What is to be in the life
of a boy has happened before.
In the same place another time.

Don't Spit on My Corner

Mi Barrio Loco

I hate my Barrio because I love her. I hate her because she can kill me. Yet, because I love her, I'll let her kill me. My Barrio is a jealous lover, she gave herself to me when I needed her. All I had to do was commit myself one hundred percent to her. My Barrio is vicious. If I don't embrace her, take care of her needs, protect her from her enemies, real or imaginary, right or wrong, she will put a jacket on me. I hate her, but I can't walk without her. I can't stand that jacket. It's a contract on my life. I don't want to die! I want to live so I can love my Barrio. My Barrio, right or wrong, still my Barrio.

∘   ∘   ∘

Psycho's car, which was a beat up 1932 Ford convertible with highly polished chrome hubcaps decided to stall in Little Eastside Gang territory. We had come to a stop sign on Brooklyn and Lorena when the motor conked out. Psycho worked on the floor starter till he killed the battery. "Dammit," he muttered, "this lousy battery cost me three bucks! The sucker told me it was good for at least six months!"

I recognized a 1937 Ford that came by with Ruben, a guy I knew, and some other guys in it. I hollered at them to come back and give us a push. They came back, parked behind us, then walked up to our car. There were four other guys with Ruben. Ruben was in the lead. He kind of swaggered over, swinging his arms, not smiling as he generally did when we met up. He was nice looking, but just now he had a hard look on his face. "Hey Ruben," I said by the way of introduction, "our car stalled. How about giving us a push?" He snarled at me, "Shut up, bitch!" and brushed past me as he looked down on David, who sat in the car acting bored by the whole scene.

Ruben hit David in the eye with his fist, opening a gash which bled immediately. The rest of Ruben's boys came out swinging and did a quick number on us.

As they drove off, Ruben hollered that our barrios were at war and that we could expect ass-kickings from now on. David hollered back, "this is the beginning, you bastards, pick a spot at the Calvary Cemetery 'cause that's where you're going to end up."

Psycho didn't seem hurt. I had some pain from a kick on the shin and spit out some blood from a cut inside my mouth. I took my handkerchief, went over to a water faucet at a nearby house, wet the handkerchief and took it back to David. "Put it on the cut and press so it will stop bleeding," I said. He did what I said without any questions. I could tell that he was pissed off. He didn't say anything. I could only guess that he was thinking of revenge. I don't know what Psycho was feeling, he just kept swearing. For myself, I was all churned up inside, fear mixing with surprise, and hoping that we could get out of there quick. We finally got a push and got the car started.

We made it up to Geraghty, as David's barrio was called, and David immediately held a council of war with some of his guys. There were five guys in the group, plus myself. I sat on the front fender of Psycho's car while the other guys sat inside.

Ganso was one of the guys listening to David talk. He was called Ganso because he waddled like a duck when he walked and flapped his arms in concert with his feelings, especially when he got excited. He was too big to be called a duck, so they called him Ganso the Goose. Right now he was waving his arms as David talked.

"I don't know what the hell started those bastards from Lil Eastside to fight with us. They said they had a beef going with us, but I didn't even know them. Only Mike knew them, so maybe it's a beef with the guys from T-Flats. I don't give a shit, though I'm gonna kick some ass."

David rarely got riled up. He was always cool, even when he got ready to kick ass. His anger was contagious, especially since these guys knew the way he was.

I remember looking around at them. I cleared my throat and reached for the quart of beer that was being passed around.

I took the quart of Eastside beer, gargled a mouthful and swallowed it. David was talking again. He said, "Hey man, if those guys want a beef, let's go get their asses. They may think they're bad 'cause they think they were just messing with T-Flats. I bet they'll really shit when they find out they were messing with Geraghty too." He had gotten up in the car while he talked. I looked at him and saw a good-looking guy who had a capacity to incite others to action just with his words.

I was witness to five guys that had pumped themselves up to mess some people up. I'd been in a few beefs up to now, but I figured they didn't compare to what was coming up, 'cause these weren't punk teenagers. These guys were streetwise and mean. "Hey, Mike, you think your boys will back us up if we go to war against those punks?" Ganso asked. Now all of them had turned and were looking at me. I fumbled with the beer bottle, took an extra long jolt, put it down and said, "Yeah, hell yeah, my boys got balls and we've had a beef going with those jerks a long time. I guess it's time we got with it and quit messing around." And suddenly I was pumped up too.

The rest of the time we spent talking and drinking. We were going to go after the guys from Lil Eastside with no mercy and no let up. David's honor was at stake and his boys would back him to the man.

The next day, the six of us packed into Psycho's convertible and cruised the Lil Eastside barrio looking for Ruben. We found him outside his house talking with some guys.

Long, lean and lanky Ganso the Goose, jumped out of the car, running and throwing bullets from a gun that materialized in his hand. David headed for Ruben, punched him, knocked him down, then slapped him, calling him a punk, daring him to fight back. The other guys had scattered but not before we could get in some licks. All the time we kept hollering, "Viva Geraghty" and "Viva T-Flats," so that they would know for sure who had messed them up.

Ruben had managed to escape from David and taken refuge in his house. He slammed the door behind him. In those days, if you made it inside the pad, you were home free. Ganso was running down the street hollering "Viva Geraghty" and shooting at the receding backs of the rest of them. He looked funny, flapping his arms and running in that goose-like way.

We laughed as we gunned the car in his direction. We picked him up and sped off. Ganso was high as a kite on the excitement. It took a long time to bring him down. Sweet revenge.

Chapter II

My father left early for work Sunday. He was working steady at this restaurant. He didn't make much, but he was working and that was dignity. He left instructions with my mother to have me take his '37 Chevy and fill it up with gas. This was okay with me 'cause he had a good car and I could take it and cruise around for a while. Maybe I could even get Penny to go for a ride with me.

I showered, checked out my shoes to see if they were spit-shined. These were French Toes, which means that the toes were square. They were black and really looked fine. Next I checked out a light grey shirt. I re-ironed the creases and when I was satisfied, I hung it up. I pulled a pair of dark grey sharkskin pants from the closet and checked them out. They were my pride and joy. I had paid $20 to have them tailor-made. These drapes really looked good, especially with that special Dutch press on the sides to make them bag out and accentuate the style which was just coming in. The bottoms were cuffed and tapered to fourteen inches. I knew I was going to look sharp today.

Before I got dressed, I got on the phone and called Penny. As I waited for someone to answer, I ran some mind pictures of Penny past my eyes. The pictures delighted me. They caught me breathing hard. What this chick could do to me was wild. Man, I'd only talked to her a couple of times. We seemed to get along well, yet this would be the first time I would try for a serious date with her. I realized that even though we had not been together that often in the past, I had still taken several mind pictures of her.

For sure, if I wanted to go steady with a chick, one that I would want to bring home to mother, one that I would ask permission to take out, one that I would walk past the guys on the corner so they could see me with class, Penny would be the one. Really, you don't have to know a girl very long to fall for her. I was living proof. This chick was cool and crazy. She went to Roosevelt High School, which was in the neighborhood. I noticed that she was quieter than the rest of the girls. She was kind of reserved, but when she talked she made sense. She was someone that made me feel like I didn't have to put on any fronts. I could be myself.

That's enough about her inner attributes. Physically, she was well put together. She had a cute little booty that wiggled from side to side when she walked, especially when she was in a hurry. Her legs weren't altogether straight, but they were full. Those white socks she wore coming out of white shoes really set them off. She wore what they called "peasant blouses." They were a bit low around the neck and fit loosely, but not so loose that they hid the firm up-tilt of a pair of knockers that were knockouts. She had a well scrubbed face, tanned instead of brown like most Mexicans. She didn't wear much makeup except for some lipstick that made her lips glow. I hadn't kissed them yet, but the anticipation was there. I knew I'd get to them no matter what else happened. It made me jealous to think some other dude might have tasted those lips before me. I was sure nobody had tasted any other part of her body, though. For sure, Penny was a virgin. That was the reason I could bring her home to mother. That was the reason I was scared of her. I wouldn't want to be the bastard that ruined her.

I had some misgivings about meeting her mother, but I promised myself I would show her all the upbringing my parents had given me. This would show her mother that Penny wasn't going out with some bum.

With the car keys in hand, I split. I started the car, then drove slowly down Grande Vista. I looked in the rearview mirror of the car towards the four-flat apartment I called home. I noticed that it wasn't bad looking, but it wasn't as nice as the house we had moved away from on the Westside of Los Angeles just about a year ago. Most of the houses on this street were single-family dwellings. They were kept up well by people who were buying after having rented for years. These homes had been occupied just a few years ago by Armenians who had since struck it rich in the trash-hauling business and were splitting for suburbia to a place called Montebello.

T-Flats territory, through which I was traveling on my way to Penny's pad, was not quite as run-down as other barrios where the *raza* lived. This could be attributed to people buying their homes and taking pride in ownership. The war economy was such that everyone that wanted to work could get a job, including housewives. Whatever they made they plowed back into their estates. Of course there were other physical aspects to T-Flats, but I didn't think about that.

I turned off the motor, looked straight ahead, grabbed the steering wheel with both hands and took a couple of deep breaths. "I wonder who I'm more scared of facing right now, Penny or her mother? Wow, what about her father, what if he's there too?" I almost started the car up and split. I was suddenly panicked, but why?

The hell with it. I got out of the car, slammed the door shut behind me and faced a small white house, well kept up, with a green lawn and flower pots by the porch. It even had a picket fence and a gate to go through. I went through the gate and up to the porch. I rapped my knuckles on the door jam and Penny came to the door almost immediately. She was all smiles. She was looking as good as my fantasies had pictured her. Maybe even better, 'cause she was standing in front of me in the flesh. I must have stared 'cause she asked me, "What are you looking at, boy?" She tilted her head back and made a delicious sound as she laughed.

I picked up that she was teasing me, probably trying to say that I wasn't as cool as I made out to be while standing around with the dudes shucking and jiving. She was right and I told her so without saying anything.

She opened the door and stood aside so I could get through. I tried not to touch her, but still managed to brush her arm and hip as I went through. "Damn, I got to be cool, did she do that on purpose? She doesn't act like it." The more I wanted to be cool, the dumber I was feeling. I felt like Mickey Rooney in the "Andy Hardy" movie series.

Penny said, "I'll call my mother so you can meet her. My father isn't here, so you can meet him some other time."

Her mother came into the front room from the kitchen,

wiping her hands on a red and white apron. Penny introduced us. She was an average-sized woman with a pleasant expression about her. I thought there was a remarkable resemblance between her and Penny. They were both good-looking, although it was obvious that Penny's mother was in her thirties, maybe even her late thirties. I liked her instinctively, which helped me to relax in front of her. She looked younger than my mother, but she dressed in the same style of clothes: not very modern but more in keeping with what the average housewife might wear who knows her place in her husband's home—the Chicano man's home, I mean. That place is to maintain the home, cook, take care of the children and be there when he needs her.

"With your permission, I'm taking Penny for a ride. We'll be back early 'cause I know it's a school day tomorrow," I said. "All right, be careful and keep your promise to have her home early." And she shooed us out the door.

We turned and walked out the door towards the car. I felt pleased with myself because I behaved in a nice way and was able to talk with some class to Penny's mother. I bet I surprised her that I could be polite and carry a conversation. It was true that I had put on drapes and my hair, which was grown out, was combed wildly in a ducktail, but I still felt good around her mother. When we got to the car I opened the door for Penny. As she got in she said, "You did all right with my mother, but she doesn't really like guys who hang around the corner or dress like you do."

This took me back. I said, "What do you mean, 'dress like me'? I'm dressed real cool, all the way down."

"You may think you look cool, but to her and my father you don't." She caught me with my tongue hanging out. I didn't know what to say. She got in the car and I closed the door behind her. I went around to my side, got in, started the motor and split for Geraghty to look for David.

I started to say something about her brother Angel, who was one of the members of T-Flats, even though he was now in the service, but I thought better of it. I figured that we might end up in an argument and I didn't need it on our first date. Instead I told her, "I'm going to drive up to Geraghty to find my friend David and his girl. Maybe they'll double date with us." I described David and his girl to her. She smiled and said it would be groovy with her. Driving to Geraghty, we made small talk about the movies, about school and about dating. I drove carefully, but not too slowly. I wondered how long it would be before I could feel safe kissing her. I made myself a promise that before this date was over, I would kiss her. I turned and smiled at her. She smiled back and said nothing. I was thinking of what a square I was becoming. Here I was betting I'd get a kiss before the day was through, while most of the time I was making bets with myself or my partners on whether or not I'd screw someone.

Unlike Geraghty, which was only a street that meandered through some hills in the unincorporated part of East Los Angeles, T-Flats had a kind of Barrio Center. T-Flats got its name from the book, *Tortilla Flats*, which was written by John Steinbeck. There was a gully called Bernal Street, which was unpaved but lined with houses which were really ramshackle. For sure, no building inspector had okayed any house down here. Nobody seemed to give a damn. Like in the book, the people were rather simple in their lifestyle. They drank home-made wine or beer and had parties that lasted for a couple of days. Everyone had dogs, cats and a large assortment of animals which produced eggs and milk, as well as meat.

Most people farmed small gardens. They grew pinto beans, potatoes, radishes and carrots. Their trees generally bore apricots and oranges. I venture to say they all had *pencas de nopales*, prickly-pear cactus. Cactus is good to eat with beans and rice. This pastoral scene prevailed until Ed Roybal became councilman of the district. One of the first things he did was have the gully asphalted.

There was generally peace among the inhabitants, broken only when some unsuspecting alien wandered in uninvited. There might be trouble unless he stated his business and it was legitimate.

Getting back to downtown T-Flats, we generally hung around in front of Lasky's Drugstore. It was on the first floor of a two-story building that was right on the corner of Fourth and Fresno. We stood here for hours watching the cars pass by, checking out who got off the streetcar. If they were nice-looking girls, sometimes we would walk along behind them until they gave us a tumble or we would walk along with them until we gave up on them.

There were several small businesses clustered on two blocks, from Grande Vista to Fresno Street along Fourth Street. There was the new Star Market, followed by Frank's Liquor Store, then Evelyn's Cafe, followed by the old Star Market, then Blanco's Barbershop, followed by Simon's Cleaner, then the Malt Shop. Across the street, still on Fourth Street, was *La Maternidad Zepeda* (a midwife service), Frontinos' Gas Station, back to Lasky's Drugstore, then Weber's Shoe Shop. Further on down the block there was Doctor Garcia's office and next to it Maria's Beauty Parlor. The reader can readily see that the T-Flats Community wanted for nothing.

We found David, Martha and Psycho on Blanchard Street. "You know, man," David said, "it's a fine day for cruising, so lets do just that."

I told him that was just fine with me, 'cause Penny and I had the same intentions. "The jefe lent me his car for the day, so let's take advantage of it."

Martha was David's steady girlfriend, if there was such a thing in his life. She was really beautiful, with big black eyes that flashed from under long lashes. Her hair was jet black and she wore it coiled on the back of her head, not like a girl but like a woman. Whenever she got excited or in the mood, she would uncoil that hair, let it hang down and swirl it. With those eyes, long black hair, light complexion and beautiful face, she could stop or start action anywhere. She was hung up on David, so she played it according to his rules. In a way I couldn't figure out why a twenty-year-old woman would want to be with a guy that had just turned eighteen.

I smiled shyly at her. She flashed me a smile in return and winked at me. She had me wondering all the time about her, 'cause she treated me in an intimate way, held my hand and made me feel special. I guess I was jealous of David because of what he had that could attract her. I figured I could always be her friend but never her lover.

But today was different, today I led Martha to the passenger side of the car and introduced her to Penny. Penny wasn't gorgeous, like Martha, but she certainly was as clean-looking. No one would be ashamed to be with her.

Penny was shy with Martha, but Martha talked with her in that special way and soon their conversation took hold.

David, Martha and then Psycho got into the back seat of my pop's '37 Chevy sedan. It was a good car, well kept inside and outside. It was his pride and joy, so I had to be careful who I hauled in it. Not everybody respected someone else's property.

It was around 2:00 p.m. on a beautiful Sunday. It made you feel good, it made you glad to be free, alive and with the girl you cared about. We were sorry we hadn't scored a chick for Psycho. Psycho said, "Don't worry, I can make out later on."

We decided to stop and get gas. While we did, David and Psycho went to the hot dog stand next door and brought back some hot dogs and sodas. Before we got started, David told me to get in back with Penny, so we could make out. He told Psycho to drive, then he climbed in the front seat with Martha.

We talked about Metro, about dances at the Sons of Herman, the fights at the Diana, the bands at the Royal Palms and the Casa Mañana. We worked with the girls on setting up dates for next weekend. They chattered on and so did I.

After a while David asked me, "Hey Mike, you got a screwdriver or any other tools?" I told him, "Yeah, the tools are in the trunk of the car." He told Psycho, "Stop the car." They got out, got a screwdriver and worked at the front and then the back of the car, taking off the license plates.

I started feeling that something was up that I wasn't being let in on. The girls kept talking, oblivious to what was going on. I went along with it. When Psycho and David got back in the car, David said, "Go ahead Psycho." He smiled at me and the girls, but talked very little. Psycho's face looked dark and grim. He looked in the rearview mirror a lot and drove very cautiously. From First Street we went over on Brooklyn and headed east towards the county line.

We got as far as Brooklyn and Evergreen and David told Psycho, "Make a left." I suddenly felt panic. We were right in the heart of Lil Eastside. What the hell were we going to do if we were recognized? There were only three of us and the girls. Those suckers would follow us and mess us up. Half way down the block, David ordered Psycho to slow down.

There were a bunch of guys standing outside a building. They were all dressed like us, in drapes which were baggy at the knee and tight at the bottom. Their hair was long on the sides and wrapped around the back in ducktails, which were kept that way with pomade or brilliantine. Any other day there would have been a variety of dress, such as Levis and khakis, along with drapes of all colors, but because it was Sunday they were wearing their best casual clothing. Suits were left for the evenings. That's when weddings, baptisms and birthday house parties and paid dances took place. The colors of their shirts were either black or maroon with long sleeves buttoned at the wrist.

They were standing around in front of a wooden building that housed a bakery and what I found out later was their club house. I could see them clearly: talking, writing on the wall and walking in and out of the building, maybe about ten of them.

"Dammit, David, what the shit you doing? Are you trying to get us done in?" All the time the girls were yakking away.

The guys saw us slow down. They stared hard at us, trying to recognize us as friends or foes. They saw the girls and figured we were friends. As we casually rolled to a stop, David spat out at me, "Get your girl down on the floor quick!" I grabbed Penny and jammed her to the floor.

David rolled down the car window, pulled out a gun that had been hidden in his jacket and calmly pulled the trigger. I heard screams from the girls and groans of surprise from the direction in which he was shooting. David finished unloading his six gun in the direction of the guys from Lil Eastside and then told Psycho to get the hell out of there.

I remember feeling an instant of sorrow for those cats. We really caught them by surprise. Some of them probably pissed in their pants; the ones who got hit were moaning. From what I could see, one was holding his arm while another was on the ground acting like he got shot in the ass. Some were just standing dumbfounded while others were hitting the dirt. There was some screaming and the loud tinkle of breaking glass as stray bullets hit the windows. The thought sped through my head that this was no movie. Funny how all kinds of stupid thoughts can crowd through your mind, making it difficult to think rationally.

Psycho drove smoothly away. He turned right two blocks down the street. He started speeding up as he went down Sloat and turned left on Brooklyn, going at an unsafe speed. I guess the immensity of it all was getting to him. I'm sure all he wanted to do now was get back to Geraghty and the safety of the hills.

The girls got back on their seats. They were gasping for air. Penny turned to me and in a near scream accused me of knowing that this was going to happen and that I had gotten her involved on purpose. She kept banging on my chest with her fists. I tried grabbing at them, and finally succeeding.

"I swear to you Penny, I didn't know they were going to shoot up that barrio. They never told me nothing." I was facing Penny in the back seat, trying to make her believe me. I must have sounded like a liar. Why should she believe me? I'd been telling her stories all along. As for Martha, David's girl, she just stared at the back of David's head as he looked out the side window. She said nothing, but you could smell her fear.

Psycho laughed wildly. It was more to ease his tension than to make fun of Penny, Martha or me. David turned around and faced us. "He's telling the truth, Penny. The kid didn't know what was going to happen. I wanted him with me when we pulled this beef because I can trust him. As for you girls, you love us the way we are or leave us. You might as well know the other side of us."

Penny and Martha stared at him. "Psycho, go by First and Rowan and let these nice chicks off. Don't forget we have dates with you next Sunday. Where do we pick you up?" I knew he was teasing them. They weren't in any mood to talk about next weekend's date. As for me, I figured we were up to our asses in alligators if the fuzz got wind of our identity.

By now Psycho was driving fretfully. Sweat was coming down the back of his neck. He was really nervous, but he did as David directed. We let the girls off on First and Rowan but not before David lectured them. "Don't tell anybody anything. You understand what I'm saying?" The girls stuttered that they understood and split.

Up on Geraghty, Psycho parked the car and got out. He

didn't say anything; he just went off walking down the hill towards the grocery store on the corner of Blanchard and Gage. I figured that he was going to buy some beer. While he was gone, I got a screwdriver and put the license plates back on the car. When Psycho got back, he had a sack with him. He drew a quart of beer out of it, put the cap next to his molar and used it as a bottle opener. The beer fizzed and made a sucking noise as the air and some beer foam were released from the bottle. I watched this procedure with a bit of fascination, wondering if I could open a bottle with my molar. I figured I would try it sometime.

Psycho took a drink from the beer bottle and then handed it over to David, who took it by the neck and drank. I no longer wondered why he didn't wipe off the top to get rid of any spittle. The fact was, that to do so was to insult the person who drank before you. You were telling him that he was unsanitary. After David drank, he handed the bottle over to me.

"Drink deep, little man, but not so much that you get drunk on us," David said and winked at Psycho who cracked up.

I guess they were trying to loosen me up, but I wasn't having any of that yet.

"Did you get scared, man?" asked David.

I spit out, "Yeah, I got scared!"

He said gently, "Well, you did all right. Look at Psycho, he's a *veterano* and he almost cracked up." Changing the subject he said, "What you gonna do now?"

I didn't look at him as I said, "I'm taking the car home and putting it in the garage. I hope nobody recognizes it while my pop is driving it." I didn't say any more, but he knew I was pissed off with him. For his part, David didn't say any more either.

It was now late afternoon. The sun was trying its best to hang around and keep things warm, but cold-looking blackish clouds kept getting in its face. It would be raining someday soon. The wind had sprung up and was making itself felt on our bodies. The long-sleeved shirt I wore did not keep the cold out adequately. I found myself wishing I'd brought a jacket.

David said, "I got to take a piss, let's go to Ganso's back yard and piss over the cliff. Nobody will see us."

Psycho and I agreed and ended up taking care of nature's

needs. I noticed in passing that anxious mothers were standing on their porches hollering at their young ones to go because it was getting dark and cold. The youngsters obeyed and soon the three of us were left alone.

I said goodbye to David and Psycho, jumped in the Chevy and drove off down the hill towards my house. As I drove, my mind flashed back on the day's events. I usually was curious about my surroundings as I drove, but not this time. I thought of what David, Psycho and I had done. It didn't matter anymore that I had just been along for the ride. The fuzz wouldn't believe me if I told them the truth. What was I talking about? This action I might repeat to my guys, but not to anyone else. David's words to the chicks came back. He had fired all the rounds in his gun and was certain that he had hit and maybe even killed somebody. That got to me. I imagined some cat laying on the ground, blood oozing through his maroon shirt, his face up towards the sky, his eyes glazed, looking at nothing. I could see his partners kneeling around him, swearing they would get revenge, asking each other if they had recognized the guys who did it and what barrio they were from. For sure, none of this would be taken lightly because hand-to-hand combat was one thing, but assassination was another. Darn, we had really started something. Again I asked myself, "Where is all this going to take us? Me, David, Psycho and our two barrios?" It was excitingly scary. I could taste the bile in my mouth and feel the sweat on the palms of my hands. My stomach didn't feel too good either. I felt like stopping and throwing up, but didn't.

I just swallowed hard. I wondered if David was cold-blooded. He hadn't shown much emotion. Would I crack and snitch if they got me? Nah, not on David or Psycho, never! Morals were one thing, but self preservation was a stronger force, especially when it was happening to me. The next several days would bear this out as I snowballed to a hell called "kicks."

On top of everything, I lost my bet with myself. I didn't get to kiss Penny—hell, she didn't even say goodbye!

Chapter III

A week later I was holding up the corner, along with other T-Flats members. We were popping polly seeds and telling war stories, which consisted mostly of love-making, gang fights and parties we had been to lately.

I had met these guys when I first moved back into the barrio almost a year ago. Actually I had known Eddie, who had been my best friend and the toughest guy in school, when we were going to grammar school. Beaver had gone to the same school, Euclid Avenue, too. I remembered him mostly as quiet, big for his age; he had the largest collection of funny books in the neighborhood. Johnny was not too much bigger than me. He wouldn't work. Instead, he depended on his mother or on his wits for money. He would shoot dice in order to get money for booze or in order to pay his way into dances.

The next was Butcher. He had two brothers already in the service. He said that was enough. Butcher didn't want to join them there. He said the good times were in T-Flats and nowhere else. He was intensely loyal to our barrio. This was one guy you could count on to back up his *camaradas*. I thought he was great and I felt bad that he would back up anybody, although a lot of times he wouldn't get the same kind of back up.

Although Tortilla Flats had about sixty guys on its informal roster, all claiming membership, the gang was divided into cliques. These guys I was horsing around with were part of a clique I belonged to.

Eddie and Johnny were talking about a house party they had been at the night before where they had gotten tore up on booze, but had scored with a couple of chicks from First Flats. They went into great detail telling us what the chicks looked like. In the middle of it all, Butcher asked them if they had screwed. They said no and started to give reasons why not. Butcher cut them off, "Don't bother me with details. If you didn't screw, you can't say anything I want to hear." The rest of us laughed and they shut up.

They asked me about the beef David, Psycho and I had gotten into with the guys from Lil Eastside. I told them a little, but not too much. I was still scared of what might be coming down. I gave David and Psycho most of the play, explaining that I was scared most of the time. Eddie said, "That's bullshit, Mike, David told us you helped him set things up and you really made T-Flats look good 'cause you went all the way." The other guys nodded their heads and slapped me on the back.

"You know, Mike, I never thought you had balls, but you got to be pretty good for those guys from Geraghty to want to hang around with you. Those are some bad dudes. I'm glad they're on our side," Beaver complimented me. This was something, coming from Beaver, 'cause he had grown big, husky and mean since we were young.

I liked these guys. They weren't as tough as the guys from Geraghty, but they were fun to be around. I could be more natural around them now, but I constantly had to prove myself. That was all right, though, 'cause they had to do the same thing. We were young, just sixteen or seventeen, barely finding our way, but we were lucky, 'cause we had each other. When we were together we could put our family problems out of our mind. So what if our fathers beat our asses, or there was no father, or our mothers liked to drink and party with strange dudes or there were too many brothers and sisters and the house was too small and we were Mexican. Hell, we were T-Flats and we had each other. Who needed more?

Two Hollenbeck police cars pulled up. The cops got out of their cars, talked with us good-naturedly about things having to do with our barrio. They asked if we were still fighting with Fourth Flats, Kern Mara and finally Lil Eastside. We told them that we had a standing beef with all of them, but we weren't fighting just now or we wouldn't be standing out in the open for everyone to see us.

They finally tired of the banter, opened the back doors of their patrol cars and told us to get in. We asked why, as we were being herded in. One of them said, "Shut up and get in." We got in. We figured it couldn't be much of a bust if they weren't putting cuffs on us. So we went along with their program.

At the station, which is located on First and St. Louis, they ordered us out of the cars. We walked from the parking lot through the back door and into the building. The outside was a big brick fortress that looked like it might have been built during the First World War. The inside looked as well used as the outside. This was my first time inside.

Most of the guys had been here before. They waved at some of the cops and the cops waved back. I was surprised at the cops' free and easy attitude.

"All right, you pachuco suckers, line up. You're going to be finger-printed and questioned," some red faced white cop hollered at us.

I continued going along with their program. I acted calm, joked with the guys and played my part. Inside I was all choked up. I wondered if these cops knew about me and my part in the shooting at Lil Eastside. They were clever, so I would have to watch what I said. I hoped that none of the guys got diarrhea of the mouth and started to brag about anything. That's how these cops got their information: suckering guys into talking and bragging about what they were up to. Me, I had already decided not to carry on any conversation with a cop.

The noise died down as we did as the policeman ordered. They filled out a card on each of us—name, address, number of arrests, convictions. Everything was matter of fact and cold. They trampled all over our rights as citizens. Who cared? So what!

During my turn at interrogation, I asked the officer, "Why are we going through this process, what are we being held for?"

His answer was simple: "Oh, you're not being busted, but sooner or later you're going to fall. We might as well save time by having you on file now. Move over here so we can get your prints. As soon as you're all processed, you'll be free to go." True to their word, they cut us loose when they were through.

Beaver asked, "Hey man, how about a ride back to the neighborhood? You brought us, now take us back."

Red Face answered, "Get your brown asses out of here before we bust you for impersonating clowns."

"Hey man," Johnny moaned, "we got to walk three miles back through some barrios who don't like us."

"That's not our problem suckers, so cut out," the cop yelled.

We cut out, but I had a feeling this would not be the last time I'd see this place. The walk back was fast and nervous. We strung out, the six of us, to make it look like there was a lot more of us. No one would mess with us if we looked like a large force. We made it without incident from First Street to Soto Street, then down some side streets to Evergreen Playground, where I had learned to swim, and over to Fourth Street and the safety of our corner.

As we walked back, I took a look at our surroundings. There were mostly homes in this area, no commercial buildings of any kind. The homes were all made of wood and had one or two bedrooms. Jews ran small businesses: the delicatessens, the bakeries, the shoe shops and the drugstores. Wherever there was a buck to be made, there were the Jews hustling to make it. The Chicanos lived in these areas in modest homes and paid modest rents. Very few owned their own homes. They were generally owned by Jews. So what, these Jews were generally pretty decent people.

This latest escapade gave us plenty to talk about and reenact when we got together with the rest of the guys afterward, but something was brewing. Those cops didn't ask any direct questions. It kind of worried the guys who were more streetwise.

I got home, got on the phone and called Penny. Believe me, it took a lot to do it, but I had to face up to it if I wanted to keep on seeing her.

The phone was answered by her mother. "What happened with you two?" she asked after I had identified myself.

"You and Penny left in such a happy mood and when she walked in the house alone she looked like she had been crying. Did you two have a fight or what?"

It was obvious that Penny had not confided in her mother. I mumbled something about us not seeing eye to eye about our dating. In order to get the weight off Penny, I told the *señora,* "We're going kind of steady and maybe I'm getting too possessive and Penny resents it. Anyway, I was calling to apologize to her."

The *señora* thought that was nice of me, but Penny had said she would not come to the phone if I called. She wanted to finish her homework undisturbed and then go to bed early. I didn't push it. I thanked her and hung up.

That was Penny, though; she didn't put any frills on her emotions. She told things straight out. Damn, that hurt, but I didn't swear at her. Whatever she laid on me I deserved.

"Ain't this a bitch," I thought. "I care for two people very much and they are at opposite poles and I try to get their approval. I wonder how I can manage Penny and her wanting me to be good and David who really doesn't ask me for anything, but expects me to be with him because I'm his partner. What a screwed up mess I'm in."

Chapter IV

I met David a few days later at Metro High after school was over. We stood around a while watching the chicks pass by. I asked him if we should pick up a couple of girls and some of the guys and go lush up. He said, "I'm not in the mood to be with too many people. Lets go off by ourselves to see a movie." I agreed and we took the streetcar downtown. It was a treat to go downtown in Los Angeles. Part of the reason was that the chicks were always around in plentiful quantities.

Instead of going to the Orpheum or the Roxy, which were barrio youth hang outs, we made it to the Paramount on Fifth and Hill Streets. They were showing "Back to Bataan" with Robert Taylor. It was another good war movie. We talked about those Americans going out in a blaze of glory. You couldn't see their bodies being ripped up by machine gun bullets, only a dense fog coming up and covering them as you heard them shouting encouragement to each other. Something like, "Long live the United States!" or did they say "*Viva mi barrio,* Down with Japan!" We laughed. Countries at war are like Chicano gangs at war. Both are patriotic, they will fight, kill or be killed to protect their established rights!

After the show, we walked down Broadway to First Street to get the "P" car. On the way there David dropped his bomb on me.

"Look man," he said, "the cops finally figured out what happened over at Lil Eastside. They're getting pretty close to figuring out who was involved because they already know that T-Flats and Geraghty had a beef going with them. I guess the only reason it took so long was because the city cops and the county cops don't get along and they don't cooperate too well. Anyway, from what I hear, there was a probation officer in the building when I shot up the place. This dude is supposed to know what is happening. I guess he wants our ass. On top of that, some cops came to my house. I wasn't there and my folks don't know nothing, so they couldn't help them."

"Psycho got busted and he's back in the Army again. He isn't going to talk and nobody knows about him, so he's clear. That leaves me and you, Shorty. What you got to say to that?"

I sucked my gut in. I had been expecting the shit to fly sooner or later, so I was prepared. I was glad it was him telling me and not some cop. "You know what, we're in it together. If we got to go, we got to go," I said, and I said it with conviction. I meant it because by now I felt that if you want to play, you have to pay, and I wanted to play.

We walked in silence for a while, then David said, "When the hammer comes down, it's going to come down on my head only. No matter what happens, you're going to be clear. There's no use in the two of us going. I don't want you busted for anything. I talked to you in a 'one way' manner just to see what you would say. You're okay, little brother!"

We got on the "P" car and headed for the city across the river. We did some talking about what might happen. There could be a chance that we could still escape, but we figured we might as well expect the worse and hope for the best. The guys that got shot were getting better. One had been hit on his right hand. He probably wouldn't be putting up any graffiti for a while. We cracked up at that. David recalled that this guy had been writing something on a wall when David had started shooting. The other guy had been hit in the ass. He had been the first to see the gun, and turned to run for the building and had fallen with a slug in his *nalgas*. That guy's feelings were really hurt. We laughed again as David recounted the story. Some guy from Lil Eastside had told David and now David was telling me.

As we hit the east side of Los Angeles, I looked out the window and noted the Christmas decorations. The night air was crisp, as it generally is in December. It was real nice outside too. I said, "I hope we all have a merry Christmas ... with our families and not in jail." David said "Amen" to that.

We started talking and making plans for where we would spend Christmas Eve and New Years. I told David that if I went off and partied, it would be the first time I didn't spend the holidays with the family.

"Look man, this is what we do on both those nights; we'll go to my house with my *gente* first and then over to yours. After that we can skip out for our own action with our chicks. Tell me, are you still taking out that square chick you had with you last time we played gangster? What I want to know is what is a cool dude like you doing with such a square?" He started to laugh.

"Ease up," I said beginning to get pissed off. "Unless you want me to start capping on your girl, you better not tell me nothing about Penny." I spat at him.

David knew he'd hit a tender nerve, so he put up his hands as if to defend himself from my fist. "How about that, little brother, you're hung up on her. Don't get upset. You two make a pair. You're both squares, only she knows she is and you don't. In a way you're a big fool for hanging around with me and playing the part. It ain't gonna get you anything but a bad time."

I had calmed down and said, "If I live to be a hundred, I won't be able to figure you out, David. You got me going, teaching me the ropes and all that jive, then you turn around and tell me I should stay a square. Why don't you make up your mind about me?" Actually, I was pleased to hear him talk this way. I knew he couldn't tell me outright that he liked me, but just by little conversations like this I got the picture. It helped to clear up in my mind why I really dug this crazy dude.

I got off the street car on First and Fresno. I watched as it rolled on with David on it. After it had disappeared, I started walking down Fresno, but not before I took a peek in the door of the corner *cantina*. It was kind of fun looking in to see what old man on his night out was making out with some old lady who was supposed to be visiting relatives some place. I was smirking at it all as I watched some dancing couples doing their thing to a Chicano tune. I felt smug because I knew my mother would never do something like that. I wondered about my father. Probably yes. He was a macho and he liked to bar hop every now and then, so he probably danced a bit too. I wondered if he ever took any action out and screwed it. He never gave any indication that he did, so I had no real way of knowing.

I made it to the apartments where we were living. Every time I started up the steps, I thought of a groovy song called "Four Flats Unfurnished." I hummed the tune now. I looked around with more appreciation, knowing that I might not be around too much longer. Being busted seemed imminent.

I shook the thought loose, walked into the apartment, said, "Hi Mama, did anybody call?" I had it in the back of my mind that one of these days Penny would break down and call me.

My mother looked at me and smiled as she brushed her hair back from her face and said, "You're home early for a change. What miracle made you come home, are your sick?" She scolded me, but gently, without answering my question about phone calls.

It really was unusual for me to come in early on a Friday night, especially since my old man didn't come in until dawn himself. He had a good excuse, he was working. She finally told me there hadn't been any calls, and she hoped there wouldn't be any 'cause they generally meant trouble for me.

"Do you want to eat?" she asked. I told her no, that David and I had eaten before I came home. I left the front room and went into my bedroom.

I turned on my record player and selected some groovy 78's to play. They were mostly jazz records featuring various artists playing crazy tenor sax, trumpet and bass. From there I progressed to some blues. The music mellowed me out. It got me thinking about Penny. I found myself comparing her with some of my other girlfriends. She was better than most of them. I wondered if she would ever talk to me again. I quickly dismissed the thought; of course she would. The days had passed since that fateful Sunday and now the weeks. After all, she might not be all that hep, but she wasn't all that square either. She knew what went on around here.

"Aw shit," I exploded at the spinning record. "What am I gonna do, spend the rest of my life crying the blues? I'm gonna wash this chick out of my mind, so I can go on living." It wasn't like I had remained celibate. I had been going out and had even gotten a piece or two, but I guess I still wanted to be up close to Penny. I decided to give it a few more days.

Christmas was coming and I wanted her to be my date. I could see David and me being with our folks and then picking up Martha and Penny and spending the rest of the evening together or, what the hell, we could pick them up first, share them with our families and then go out. Yeah, that would be great!

The phone rang around noon the next day. Momma came in and said it was for me. "My, are we getting to be a lover boy. The girls are even calling us now." She teased me and I told her to knock it off, but in a nice way. I wondered who was calling me.

"Hi, it's me. I wonder if you could come over today and see me?" I almost choked, my mouth dried up and I got a buzzing in my head. It was Penny. It was she's-so-fine Penny. It was I-like-your-moves Penny.

I was finally able to say, "Yeah, I can come over. What time would you like to get together with me?" She told me it was twelve, so one-thirty would be okay with her, if it was okay with me. I agreed immediately.

By one-thirty I was parked in front of her house in my 1930 Model A Ford two-door sedan. This car was an absolute wreck that needed tires, but it did have a good motor. My father had bought it for me for $35. This sounds like a good deal, but my father sold my '34 Ford, which was a real cherry, because, as he claimed, I got a ticket. He pocketed the profit. I had a quiet fit, but said nothing. He was the Man and I respected that without knowing why.

I started to get out to get Penny from the house, but she beat me to it. She came out of the house, walked down to the car and climbed in. She closed the door behind her and sat there for a minute. "Hi," she said.

I asked her, "You want to go to the Warner Brother's Theater?" This show was in downtown Los Angeles on Seventh and Hill Streets. They always showed good movies. "They're showing 'Gentleman Jim Corbett' with Errol Flynn. It's about boxing."

Penny was game. I started the Model A's motor and waved goodbye to her mother, who had come to the door. She waved back and I drove off. As we drove along Fourth Street on our way downtown, we talked.

We got down to what had happened that crazy Sunday. There was no use trying to defend my actions to her. She was too cool for that. I went into a detailed account of what life in the barrio was all about. Towards the end of my account I looked over at her. She had been listening politely, but it seemed to me with no great interest. I decided to change the subject.

I asked her, "Why haven't you returned my calls? You must have known I'd never mess you up on purpose. I got to admit I'm close to being hung up on you. I know I got no control over you and, yes, I date other chicks, but I'll knock it off if you want to go around with me." My proposal to go steady sounded almost like a proposal of marriage. I hoped I didn't sound like a big fool begging for anything, but I knew I did.

She looked straight ahead as she answered my request to go steady. "Mike, I like you very much, in spite of your way of life. I'll go around with you, but you have to promise not to involve me in anymore of your gang's activities. I really don't want to know what you do."

I took my eyes off the road long enough to smile at her. We smiled at each other. "Wow, we're going steady." I didn't promise her anything, but I promised myself that I would be good to her.

We made it inside the Warner Brothers. It was a classy theater. Nobody from the barrios went there. During the movie I looked at her while she looked at the screen. She really seemed to concentrate and we talked very little. We sat in the center section and in the center of the theater. No backseat in the side aisle for us. I not only was dressed square, I was acting square with her. I caught myself cracking up on myself. "Look at me acting like I did on my first date back so long ago."

As we sat there watching the movie, I moved my hand over and tentatively reached for hers. She had her hand in her lap and made no attempt to reach for mine. I found myself being rebuffed, but not in the sense that she didn't want to hold my hand, more like she was extremely shy or fearful of meeting me half way. I asserted myself and took her hand in both of mine in a gentle but firm manner and pulled it towards me. I brought her fingers up to my lips and kissed them one at a time. The good feeling was there for me and I knew the same was happening to her, even though we didn't talk. We sat through a damn good show, which we both enjoyed. I also fell in love.

We didn't talk much while I drove her home. She stroked the fingers of my hand almost absentmindedly as we rode to her home. She might not have felt anything, I don't know, but I certainly did. I parked in front of her house, stopped the engine and sat there waiting for her to move. She didn't move or say anything. "What the hell should I do now?" I couldn't figure where I stood with her. She didn't give me any hints as to how to act. "Aw crap," I thought. I got out of the car, went around to her side to open the door for her. She had opened it herself and gotten out. Was she playing independent? Was she telling me to get lost? I just couldn't figure her out.

"Thank you for a nice time, Mike. I really enjoyed being with you." She faced me and smiled. Her eyes kind of sparkled and her lips curled up.

I knew she meant it. I moved close to her almost involuntarily. I held her face in my two hands and kissed her. She kissed me back. It was awkward for her because she didn't know how to kiss very well, but wow! She kissed me back and that was something. I turned her loose and she went inside the house. As for me, I stood there like a big fool trying to sort things out. I couldn't do it. I made it to the car and drove on down to the corner.

I hit the corner, just to see if anyone was around, kind of out of habit. Some of the guys were holding up the corner. I decided not to stop. I wasn't up to it. Could you believe it? A date to the show with a girl who was square and I didn't even have a drink. I felt good, I'd finally been kissed. My fantasy was reality?

Before I'd gotten her home, I asked Penny to go out with me on Christmas Eve and said that David and Martha would be with us. I told her that I hoped that this would not make a difference. She told me that I had a right to my friend. David frightened her, but she liked Martha. She would have to ask her parents and then she would give me her answer. She admitted that she had always spent Christmas with the family. I told her that I understood, 'cause if she said yes, it would be my first time out and away from my family too.

This was Sunday, Christmas Eve was three days away on Wednesday. I had things to do. Penny had promised an answer by tomorrow night. David was going to check out what his parents were going to do and I had to do the same thing. We had decided to go into town after work on Monday and pick up some clothes we'd ordered.

"Mama, what have you and Papa set up for Christmas Eve?" I asked as soon as I had walked in and said hello to her. "Well, *hijo*," she answered, "we probably are going to get together here with your aunt and uncle. They will bring the children. Why do you ask?"

I didn't know how to approach it, so I busied myself heating up a tortilla. While I did this I got some frijoles and a piece of cheese. When the tortilla was warm, I put the beans and cheese in it and rolled it up. I got a paper napkin and wrapped it around the tortilla so as not to dribble anything on the floor. In the meantime, Mama got me a glass of milk from the refrigerator. While going through this ritual, I told her that I wanted permission to go out Christmas Eve. I asked her if I would have any trouble with my father. To tell the truth, I think I surprised her by asking permission and going into detail as to what I expected to do. By the time I had scarfed up my burrito and drank my milk, Mama and I were in agreement. I even went so far as to ask her to ask Papa for the use of his car. Man, if he would lend me his car, it would really make for a memorable Christmas.

I went to the window, opened it up and asked her if she thought it would snow. We both laughed. It was a near cinch it wouldn't snow, it probably wouldn't rain, but late at night it might get cold. What a crazy country. It seemed like it was always either hot or warm. Christmas in Los Angeles was not like Christmas anywhere else. We might sing the winter songs and expect Santa to be bundled up for cold, but we had a hard time believing it. Mama and I shared this observation.

Monday I got up early, washed, dressed in Levis, ate breakfast prepared by my mother and left for work. I took the streetcar to work because it was easier to travel that way; parking the car would be a drag.

Lockheed was a big aircraft factory that had opened up a lot of little sub-plants like the one that had hired me. Before the war, airplanes were made in huge factories on the outskirts of town. It was hard for the average person to get to work, so close-in sub-plants had sprung up to accommodate a work force made up of youngsters, housewives, 4-F's and returning service veterans. This plant was located just on the western end of the Seventh Street bridge on the corner of Seventh and Santa Fe. Their main product was P-38 airplane wings and tails. I started out bucking rivets at sixty cents an hour. When I quit, I was making a dollar an hour as a riveter. Believe me, this was good wages for a seventeen-year-old.

After work, as we had agreed, David and I got the R street-car downtown. We shopped around for gifts for our families. He bought a necklace for Martha, which I was sure would set off her neck and dress and would draw attention to her nice knockers. I was more practical. I bought Penny a chenille robe. I figured she would like it, and that she would remember me every time she put it on. I just hoped it wasn't too personal. What the hell, though, wasn't she going around with me?

Since it was still early, we decided to treat ourselves to something to eat in a good Paddy place for a change. For the times, there was nothing better than Clifton's Cafeteria on Fifth and Broadway, so that's where we went. Most of the people were dressed in suits and going out dresses. We were in Levis, but we felt honorable because we were working men doing our thing for the cause.

I'd only been to Clifton's once or twice and considered it a real classy place. It had waterfalls and different areas to eat in, once you got your food, which you got cafeteria style. This was my introduction to Lobster Thermador. I liked seafood, but had never had anything like this before. I don't remember what David had, but what I had really got to me. It sure was good.

Later, we walked down Main Street, boarded the F streetcar across the Fourth Street bridge to Fourth and Fresno. I let David go on home and I walked from Fourth and Fresno to my home. Mama checked me out, "You're getting awfully thin, you better start living a slower, more sane life." She got me thinking. "Maybe I should work out to build up my muscles." I wondered what I would look like fat? I puffed up my cheeks and checked them out in the mirror. "Shit," I thought, "I'll never be fat."

The phone rang, my mother hollered for me to hurry, a girl wanted me on the phone. I took the phone from her and asked, "Hello?" It was Penny. She told me she had called two times, that it really wasn't nice for a girl to call a guy, but she had good news and wanted to share it with me. Yeah, I had guessed right. I could take her out, she could stay out until 2 a.m., which was really something. "Oohee," this was really fine. I was one happy dude. I told her I loved her and would call her the next day. Here, at the pad, I knew I wouldn't take no for an answer. My father might not lend me the car, but there was always the Model A.

Tuesday passed and now it was Wednesday, December 24. All this day was a busy one for me. I was trying very hard to keep things cool at home in order not to get my father out of sorts. My mother was on my side, mainly because I had confided in her. Johnny and Butcher had called to ask if I was going to party with them. I had to tell them that I had a date and was going to double up with David. That softened it for me, because David was no one to mess with. I promised to get to Butcher's house if I got out of my date early enough. This seemed to placate them.

That evening, after promising my father that I would be very careful driving his car, he teasingly handed me the keys. I headed for David's house. The deal was that we would begin at David's house, visiting first with his parents. Next we would pick up Penny and visit with her parents, then over to my home. When we had covered all our bases, we would end up at Martha's place, where we were invited to a late party with young folks. I was looking forward to one hell of a time.

I knocked, then walked into David's house. His mother and father were in the front room talking when I walked in. I went over to Don Emilio and shook his hand, then I went to Doña Esther, hugged her and wished her a merry Christmas. I never drank liquor in front of them and they didn't offer me any. Instead we sat and talked while I looked around. They didn't have a tall Christmas tree, just a small one on top of a table. There were lights on it that blinked on and off and presents around it. They would be given out later that night or the next day.

David came into the room. He was ready to leave. I checked him out. He was wearing a brown sharkskin suit, a white shirt with French cuffs and a solid brown tie which was tied in a Windsor knot. The collar of his shirt was spread. His shoes were brown with French toes. He was looking damn good. One reason I approved was I had been with him when he went to Murray's Men's Clothes. As a matter of fact, I helped him pick out his clothes. One thing for sure, when we ordered our clothes, I made sure we wouldn't pick the same color or style.

"Hey, David," I said, "you sure look clean tonight. You won't have trouble keeping Martha, but if you lose her, you're looking so fine you could make out right away." We laughed at each other and I waited for his reaction to my clothes and the way I fit them.

"You look sharp tonight, *chaparro.* Your girl is going to fall in love with you all over again."

His parents agreed. I blushed and secretly agreed with them, even though David had called me "shorty" in a friendly way. We had ordered these clothes at Murray's two months ago. The suits were tailor-made and had cost each of us $85 to get them the way we wanted them. I had gotten a blue serge suit. It was a single-breasted two-button roll with wide lapels. My pants were cuffed and had conservative eighteen-inch bottoms. I wanted to be cool regardless of where I was. Like David, I was wearing a solid-colored tie and a shirt with French cuffs. I kind of liked wearing cuff links. They made me feel rich.

We stayed at David's home for about a half hour more, then said our goodbyes for the night. As usual, David's mother told him to be careful and to take care of me. I stood by and blushed as usual. Don Emilio waved us out. "I know you're going to have fun, so I'll ask you to be careful wherever you go," he said. We promised to do right and hurried on out to the car.

"You feel like drinking something before we get to Penny's house?" David asked. I told him no. I didn't want to get there with anything on my breath. "You know me, I'll take a couple of drinks and get high off of nervousness. I don't want any of that till after we get out of my house." He just sat back and laughed. "Okay partner, we're going to be a couple of clean dudes tonight, at least till after we get through the family thing. After that, let the good times roll," and he rolled his shoulders as I glanced over to him and smiled in anticipation.

We knocked on the door of Penny's house. As we waited for her to answer, I wondered how Penny would react to seeing David in person again. They hadn't seen each other since that "bad news" Sunday. Doña Ramona came to the door, looked at us, recognized me and said, "Come on in, don't stand out there, it's cold." We thanked her, walked in and I introduced David. Penny walked over to us. She smiled warmly at both of us. That took care of my worry. She leaned over and quickly kissed my cheek. I moved in and then back, I didn't want to mess things up. I was just plain scared in front of her folks. David looked cool and kind of smiled down at me. I couldn't figure out if it was a wise, big brother smile or a "making fun" of me smile. Who cares! I shined it on. Penny took us around and introduced us to her family. I didn't really pay attention to any of them, although I remember being polite. I felt secure because I was dressed right. We finally left Penny's home. Her parents didn't give me a time to bring her back, but I gathered that about 2 a.m. would be acceptable. I felt good that they would trust me with their only daughter and, no matter what happened tonight, I wouldn't screw things up.

The three of us piled into the front seat of the Chevy and we were off to my pad. By this time I could feel David's vibes because they were like mine. We were getting our family obligations over with, then we could be free to be us.

At my home, I introduced Penny for the first time to my father and mother. They were impressed with her. I guess they were expecting a *pachuca* to be my date. I sure got a kick out of her charming them. It was good to see them looking at me as if I had good taste.

To tell the truth, I had fallen in love again, only this time with a woman. I had seen Penny dressed in short skirts and blouses with white shoes and socks, a nice looking high school student. Tonight I walked out of her household with her in a light blue dress that fell to her knees. It clung to her hips, was tight around a small waist and blossomed out to meet well

proportioned breasts. The dress at this point came to a V at
the cleavage. It was not suggestive, it was just plain, naturally
revealing. She was looking innocently provocative, ripe but
innocent. I had looked her over in her home and I looked her
over here in my home and felt proud. I knew that if David
teased me, from now on it would be with respect for my taste!

My mother took Penny by the hand and introduced her
around to the other members of my family. Tio Chio and his
wife Jesusita, Tio Manuel and his wife Manuela, all made her
over. They had seen me born and they had seen me growing
up. They were now seeing me with the first girl I had ever
brought home. I wondered if they thought I was still a cherry.
They probably did. All of my aunts and uncles had been born
and raised in Mexico. They had migrated to Los Angeles in
the 1920's and had been here ever since. They, like my Ma
and Pa, had been working and trying to raise their children.
As long as they had been here, they were still strangers. They
didn't speak English and shunned having to do anything with
English-speaking people, if they could help it. They were generally ill at ease in front of Anglos, but pushed hard to get their
children integrated and be a part of the Anglo action. It was
strange, their feelings, but I wasn't trying to figure things out
this night. All I wanted was some good times. I was pointing
for it and I knew that tonight would be something to remember.

We were finally able to leave my family, but not before my
father attempted to bestow manhood or peerhood on me. He
offered me a glass of wine and also one for David. I declined,
although I didn't want to. This was something to think on. I
told him that I was driving and had responsibility for Penny
and David, plus his car. He agreed and said we would save
the glass of wine for some other time. I think he wanted to
show his brothers that his son had come of age and he was
recognizing it by allowing his son to drink with them. I hoped
I hadn't blown it for him. David had no qualms. He did what
I would have done. He drank not only one but two full glasses
of Dago Red and smiled at me. I smiled back.

And now, at last, we were on our way. "How fine." I
wanted to explode with joy. Instead, I threw the keys to the
car at David and directed him to drive. "You know the way

to Martha's better than I do. Besides, I want to finally put my arms completely around this beautiful woman and not let go all night long." They both laughed at me. David did as he was told. We got in the car and we were off at once to Martha's pad and a good time. True to my word, I put my arms around Penny. She didn't resist, she cuddled herself in as close as possible. "Is that your heart banging away?" she teased. I teased back, "Naw, it's yours, we're so close you can't tell the difference."

I looked up from a couple of fierce, French-tongued kisses long enough to check on what the "poor people" were doing on the streets tonight. At eleven o'clock at night, nearing one hour to midnight and Christmas, there was plenty of activity. It seemed that everyone on First Street was going someplace or coming from someplace. It didn't matter much if they were walking, driving in private cars, or riding the streetcars. I wondered briefly what servicemen were doing on a night like this. I could see myself in a uniform wandering into a USO, playing the part of a lonely soldier away from home and having some young Paddy chick come on to me, hoping to make it easier for me. All these quick fantasies were the consequences of watching war movies with the common soldier in the role of the hero.

David drove the car slowly past Martha's house. There was a parking space in front, but he made no attempt to park there. Penny wondered why.

I explained, "We never know what's going to happen at a house party. You don't want your car to be a victim of someone not liking you."

Penny shook her head.

"What's bothering you?" I asked.

She replied, "Don't you guys ever relax? This is Christmas, everyone is happy. Everyone wants to have a good time. No one wants to mess things up."

David and I agreed with her that nobody wanted to mess up, but we were just being careful and cautious, no use taking any chances.

David parked the car, got out and started walking back to Martha's house. This left Penny and me alone to trade spit and say our "I love yous" in private. We started breathing heavy, so I broke it off. For one thing, I didn't want any passion cramps and, for another, I didn't expect to score, nor would I attempt it. So the best thing to do was to go inside that house and boogie.

As we walked towards the house, I tried to clean the lipstick off my face. I finally asked for help and laughingly got it. She stared intently at me as she performed the clean-up job. I looked at her and felt myself melting and my legs actually buckling. "You sure are fine," I said.

She said, "Thank you," almost coyly. "When I get in the house, you'll have to tell me where the bathroom is so I can straighten out."

I agreed, but felt that she was as straight as could be already.

Martha and David met us at the door. They stood looking at us with big grins. David had probably told Martha a couple of things about us. He probably said I was acting like a maniac with Penny, after having to contain myself in front of the families.

"Hi, Mike," Martha said, and hugged me. "Merry Christmas for now and for later too." I returned the hug and the greeting.

"Hi, Penny." Martha hugged her too and also said, "Merry Christmas. Come on in, you two, and get started. We have a fine dance going on now.

We walked in with Martha leading Penny toward the bathroom. David and I looked at their receding booties with unveiled admiration. These tomatoes were really fine. Martha already knew it by the way she walked and dressed. In time Penny would come to know it about herself too. We eased ourselves around couples doing the "pachuco stomp," as I called the Chicano way of jitterbugging, and we found our way to the kitchen and the liquor.

"Hey, buddy, what do you want to drink?" David asked me as he shouldered a dude out of the way.

"Give me beer for now, but make it a Lucky. I don't like Eastside, especially if I have a choice," I said.

He handed me a Lucky and took one for himself, then we walked from the kitchen back to the front room. I looked around at the guys dancing or talking with their chicks. I guessed everybody came with a date because everyone seemed paired off. There were about twenty couples, most of them from Geraghty. Ganso was there in his sharkskin suit, waving his arms like a goose flapping his wings as he danced his own version, making up steps as he went along. His girl suffered through it all good-naturedly.

Finally Martha and Penny reappeared. Penny was looking even better than when she left me. This was due, no doubt, to some beauty tips from Martha. They came up to me and Martha said, "Mike, your girl is beautiful and sharp too. You take care of her or I'll spank you. She poked the dimple on my cheek, which showed when I smiled. She left us and glided over to David, while I stood and inhaled the perfume she left in her wake.

I turned back and smiled at Penny. "Martha sure is fine, isn't she?" I said.

Penny agreed, but said, "I'm kind of jealous of her. She's so beautiful and cool, she makes me feel plain. But then, she's so friendly, you can't help but love her right off."

I agreed.

They played a slow record, so we went out to dance. The record was mellow and easy to follow. We danced about three straight pieces, then took time out. I drank a couple more beers while Penny drank some punch. I started getting a little fogged up, so we decided to get some air on the porch. There were some other couples with the same intentions. We said our hellos and found a spot to sit on the porch steps. I put my arm around Penny and held her close to me. She shivered and I suddenly picked up that it was colder than an ice box.

We decided to go sit in the car. It would be warmer there. We got in the front seat. I put on the radio. They played some soft music and then some Christmas songs. We really didn't pay too much attention because we were busy hugging and kissing once again. I started to lay her down on the seat, but I stopped myself, leaving her gasping. I wasn't ready for this with Penny and I wasn't about to treat her like she had no class. I leaned over, opened the door and told Penny to get out, we were going back to the dance.

I hurried her back in the house. I had sobered up, but needed a drink after that last bit of action. I felt like some fool trying to shield Penny from what comes naturally once both of you agree to make it together. I suffered later from passion cramps, but I kept her chastity intact.

We danced again. A few fast pieces and a couple of waltzes and the time ran out on us. I told David that I was going to split so I could get Penny back on time.

He said, "You're having a good time, stick around."

I said, "I don't want to mess things up for us for the future. Do you want to leave too?"

He told me, "I'll get a ride back later. The party is really rocking and there is no reason to split."

I figured that David would be staying with Martha tonight. Tomorrow she would find him in her stocking for sure. The thought made me hurt in the groin, especially since all I would get tonight was a kiss, a thank you and a good night. That was my problem, though, because that's the way I wanted it.

Penny and I thanked Martha and said good night to anyone who looked our way as we walked out. David called out as we walked toward the car, "You and Penny take it easy, and I hope Santa brings you what he's bringing Martha and me." He cracked up and whacked Martha on the butt at the same time. She cracked up along with him. Ganso stood on the porch holding a quart of beer in one hand and waved his other arm at me honking, "Merry Christmas, fools."

I drove off with Ganso's bellowing in my ears. I was half loaded, happy and utterly at ease. I hoped that Penny felt the same. I drove carefully and got her home before the witching hour. Boy, did I feel proud of myself.

She kissed me good night, told me, "I had a wonderful time. I'll be your girl if you still want it that way."

My heart was full as I drove off. I felt as if my problems were over. With Penny next to me, I wouldn't have to get into anything stupid anymore.

I didn't go to Butcher's house. I'd partied enough for one night. No use pushing a good thing too far.

Chapter V

"Hey, Mike, some white guy came by looking for you a little while ago." This was hollered at me by Johnny as I reached the corner of Fourth and Fresno where Marty's Malt Shop was. The guys were hanging around the outside doing what they did naturally—nothing.

I became wary and asked who the white guy was, what he wanted, what he looked like, where he was from. The guys said he was tall, could have been a cop dressed square, was about thirty and talked in English.

"When did he ask for me exactly?" I asked. The real facts were that the man had not really asked for me, but since he asked funny questions, they weren't going to answer him. Instead, they figured the "judge" should talk to him. I was the "judge" on occasion because of my gift of gab, especially when it came to talking in English.

Johnny said, "The white dude said he'd be back later this afternoon. We want you to talk to him."

Three o'clock was a good time to stand around Marty's Malt Shop, because the girls started passing by on their way home from school. They would come swinging down in pairs. We would shuck with them, then invite them in for a soda and a quick dance. Oh, we were the killers, all right. These girls were always being warned by their parents not to pass Marty's, to keep their eyes down if they did, and never, never to talk to the pachucos standing on the corner because they were no good.

Bees to honey is what it was. Those little girls came by and were charmed by us no-goods. When they got together later on and compared notes, it was like having tested forbidden fruit for them. How about us? We felt like lady-killers till we fell for one of those broads. Then like all mortals, we became mere slaves. Many a good strong dude was lost because some sweet little tomato with innocence came along and took him away. This was how it had happened to me with Penny and that was for sure, man.

The record player was blowing loud and clear. They were mostly fast records by black musicians and some swing stuff by white bands, but nothing Mexican.

The place filled up with guys and girls. Some were meeting for the first time, others were setting up dates for the weekend. They were making collections for sodas, they were listening to gossip, they were dancing, they were standing alone.

We started in the door but stopped and looked as a car came around the corner from Fourth Street to Fresno, slowed down and finally stopped.

Johnny nudged me, "That's the man that came earlier. You want to walk up to him or make him come to us?"

I didn't have to decide, because he got out of his car and started across the street. On the spur of the moment, we decided to meet him, turn him around and let him sit with us on the lawn across the street. If this was barrio business, we didn't want non-barrio people in on what he might be here to say.

I checked him out as we walked across the street. He was big, lean and had on slacks that ran straight down with no cuffs or peg. He wore a tweed jacket with elbow patches and a dress shirt with a straight collar and a tie that wasn't all the way up snug. He looked casually cool, but in a Paddy way, you know, like out of *Esquire* magazine. I didn't check his face because I wasn't ready to look in his eyes.

We waited for him to begin talking as we surrounded him and led him to the lawn to sit down. He said, "My name is Pasterman, Leo Pasterman. I'm a probation officer. I'm worried because there's so much gang activity. Juvenile Hall, County Jail and the hospitals are full of your kind and I want to help stop all the negative action. That's why I'm here."

There were all kinds of reactions to what he had to say, such as, "If you got nothing official, get your ass out of here. You ain't nothing but a cop. If we told you anything, you'd bust us. When did anyone decide to give a damn about us? You been going from barrio to barrio. I bet you talk bad about our kind all around—now you're starting with us."

He listened to all the negative garbage we could throw at him. He seemed straight, but then everybody seemed straight when they were out to get you. For my part, I joined in the negative, I wasn't about to admit to anything—not even my name.

He got up, said, "I'll be coming around again. I hope you think over what I said." He put out his hand. No one shook it. He looked at it and put it down. I'm sure he blushed. If it had been me, I know I would have.

After he drove off, the guys laughed about what he had to say. It went deeper, though. All of us were snowballing to jail. All of us had been involved in something they could send us away for. I had finally met the probation officer who was supposed to have been in that Lil Eastside Clubhouse when we shot it up. I didn't cop to the guys or to Pasterman. I wondered if he'd made me. This barrio had been lucky that the cops had not come down on us harder. Other barrios were getting their dudes busted and sent away for nothing—just to get them off the streets. I heard that three guys from Lil Eastside who I knew from Metro High were sent to Preston, which is a state reformatory, just for writing their names on walls.

Meanwhile, gang activity had really escalated. We couldn't walk the street at night anymore. We couldn't stand around the corner without posting sentries, because carloads of guys were always coming by looking for trouble. We gave a lot, we took a lot.

Pasterman kept coming around the neighborhood on a regular basis. He offered to take us on outings. He wanted us to start a club so that we could do things that were more socially acceptable. We went on the outings and managed to mess up his plans with our lousy way of acting. We would sneak booze along, get drunk and make life miserable for him. I guess he had a mission to accomplish, because he hung in there with us. Some of the guys figured him for a softy, because he kept turning his cheek. They wanted to punch him out once and for all. I guess he had gotten to some of us, because we voted against it.

We started going to Evergreen Playground. Some of the

guys and girls made arrangements with the coach to use a room for club meetings and then we would play football afterwards. We filed into the meeting room one night and noticed that someone had written "Excelsior Club" meeting.

Art picked up an eraser. "We didn't vote on that name. We don't know what it means and it'll have to go." He erased the blackboard and wrote "Tortilla Flats."

"Who crossed out 'Excelsior,'" asked the coach.

"We did," we said, and that was the end of the club. The coach thought he was bad, because he chased us out. He never knew how lucky he was that no one decided to *rat pack* his insensitive ass.

Chapter VI

One night we were standing around the corner of Fourth and Fresno. There must have been about fifty guys. There was nothing solid, but we expected the guys from Lil Eastside to pull a raid. Let them, we could kick their asses with this many guys. There were some rifles stashed and the guys who would use them stayed close by them.

A car came east on Fourth Street, turned the corner and kind of slithered to a stop. One of our guys pulled out a rifle, then another two guys went to check out the occupants. There was only one guy, that crazy Pasterman again.

David asked him what he wanted. "I want you guys to listen to me for a while. You guys may not believe it, but the other day when you shot up the clubroom, I was in there talking to those guys about a truce meeting. You're lucky nobody is dead. Anyway, the cops are going to declare war on all "Zoot Suit hoodlums." That means you're going to land in jail just for wearing a ducktail. What I want to do is get all the gangs together for one big meeting. At the meeting we can iron out difficulties between the gangs. I can even have lawyers there for you, in case any of you get busted for any gang activities. I know the cops are getting warrants for the arrest of guys from most all the gangs in E.L.A. Will you guys participate in a truce meeting if it's set up?"

We stood around thinking out loud about it. Finally, Art said, "Look Pasterman, if you get barrios like First Flats and Kern Mara to show up, then we know you got pull and maybe we'll show up too." Yeah, that was a good answer. There was no use having a truce meeting with only the small gangs there, because the big gangs generally dictated what would be, anyway. Flats and Kern were always at each other for any number of reasons. If they could meet at the same time, maybe things would cool down.

Chapter VII

The day of the big truce meeting was set for Saturday morning about three weeks after Pasterman came by. It was held in the meeting room of the Housing Authority Office in Aliso Village.

Something like fifteen gangs sent representatives as spokesmen. I was picked because I could speak and understand the Paddy English. Two others, Beaver and Art, who were real leaders, would guide me if I needed it. David and Ganso represented Geraghty. We sat next to some guys from Lil Eastside. This one guy, Indio, talked easily to David, but kept glaring at me. Since he wouldn't talk to me, I shined him on and talked to Beaver. Beaver told me that Indio was a punk and if things didn't come off right, he was going to kick his ass right there. I told him to be cool, because we were on our honor.

The meeting began, but not until friends had shaken hands, adversaries of bygone fights had nodded respectfully to each other and everyone had checked the exits and entrances and the faces of the whites to see if they smelled like cops or fingers. Pasterman asked that the white men at the head of the table identify themselves. They were mostly practicing attorneys who said they would handle all cases that were pending. They would pay bail and be trial lawyers, if it came to that.

Pasterman asked permission to speak. This was agreed to, and he spoke of gang fights, killings, jail sentences, crying parents, downing of the *raza* in the eyes of the system. Everything we did was senseless he said, but he was careful not to sound condemning, condoning or condescending. I felt a great deal of admiration for him that day. That crazy Jew really had his guts, putting all this dynamite in one room and then striking a match. "What if these stupid gunsels didn't catch the intent of his words?"

50

A guy named Lolo from Flats followed up on Pasterman's speech. He was a heavy with much *respeto* in most barrios. He said, "I'm for Pasterman and what he wants to do, which is to start a Council of Barrios, stop the fighting wherever possible, build up the *raza* instead of bringing it down. We need to have social activities as well as recreational activities."

Conrado from Kern said, "I doubt if it can happen overnight or that it can last, 'cause there's so many young *locos* who don't understand and they're looking to make a name for themselves." He took a deep breath, then said, "My barrio is honorable, we'll give it a try."

With Lolo showing the way, the other representatives of the gangs present agreed to basically the same thing, that it was stupid to be fighting with each other for nothing, really. But they didn't fall in easily. Some of the guys from Lil Eastside wanted revenge from Geraghty and T-Flats for the raid we had pulled. David got up and said, "That's bullshit, if you hadn't started the whole beef, there wouldn't have been any raid." He glared in their direction as he talked and he made them back down. The guys from Kern and El Hoyo Mara said they would be cool if First and Fourth Flats would be cool too. They heard what Lolo had said and liked his style.

For my part, it all reminded me of a lot of Indian tribes sitting around a fire, first bringing up all the past trespasses against each other, then looking for honorable solutions and smoking the peace pipe. The only added ingredient was the presence of the white man with his eternal righteousness. Who was Pasterman? Gary Cooper? Standing tall among the noble savages? What movie was this taken from? Talk about fantasies! But this really was happening.

A deputy district attorney had some warrants to serve. If the guys were there and would identify themselves, they would be placed in custody, but their attorney would be with them right from the start and without pay. He read off some names. After the meeting broke up, some guys surrendered themselves. David went too. I stayed with him till a Mr. Gallagher took his case. Then they took him away. I was ready to bawl. David told me, "Be cool and stay that way and don't say nothing to anyone. This thing has been hanging over me long enough, but there is no way I want you to take a fall too. Come see me soon."

They lodged him in the County Jail. I figured I wouldn't
see him on the outs for a long time, and I prayed that this
whole thing wasn't a big frame-up. I knew how the Indians
felt when the Great White Father pulled his number on them.

I got a letter from David while he was in the County Jail.
They didn't take him to Juvie, they figured he was too "high
power" because his beef was attempted murder. The letter
read like this:

> "Dear Mike, things aren't that bad here. They
> have us segregated, the Chicanos in one tank, the
> Blacks in another and the Paddys in another. This
> way there is no fighting among us. I never figured
> there was racial problems among people who be-
> longed to the law.
> "I wrote the words to a song which isn't popu-
> lar, but I liked it. Learn the words, you'll like it too.
> The name of the song is 'Hurry, Hurry Baby.' It's
> a lament by a girl for her soldier who's off to war.
> She'll be true because he was the only one, but for
> him to hurry back quick, 'cause she had a terrible
> need for him. I wonder what the terrible need could
> be. Ha Ha! I bet she was just shucking him in or-
> der to make him feel macho. Look in on Martha.
> If you can, help her in any way. I would appreci-
> ate it. She visited me and talked of marriage. I'm
> thinking I might do it if I still have a job after I get
> out of the bucket. I think she's pregnant, but she
> only hinted at it. Give my regards to Penny. Stay
> close to her, but not too close, and if you do get that
> close, take precautions or else I'll end up being your
> *compadre*. Well, see you soon. Take care and take it
> easy, Greasy. You have a long way to slide. David."

I went to visit David. I had to walk into a noisy visiting
room, get on the elevator and go up to the eleventh floor. I
got a silent kick out of the name they gave the County Jail:
the "Grey Bar Hotel." Visiting people in jail was new to me.
It was confining, to say the least. All eyes, especially those
of the cops, seemed to be on me while I was there. People

waiting to see their visitors stared at me also. It seemed like they wondered about you.

I found out later that in the County Jail, the courts and offices were below the tenth floor, while the jail occupied the tenth through the thirteenth floors. It had a special section for juveniles who might be too hot to handle in Juvie. David was right.

As I said before, visiting people in jail was new to me, but it probably wouldn't be for long, not the way things were going and the way I was acting. I could bet and win that I would be seeing more of my *camaradas* in here as time went by and, sooner or later, I would be looking out from the screen that separated us at somebody from the neighborhood or my parents. What a drag. I sure didn't want my folks in on what I was up to, but I sure wasn't thinking about changing my life style either. It was too groovy.

David asked, "How are things on the outs? Has the truce been kept?" I told him, "The guys still give each other bad looks at school, but nobody has pulled anything stupid." Now that revenge was out of David's system, he liked the idea of being able to get along with the *batos* from other barrios. I knew I liked the idea, too. He laughed 'cause I was always getting caught out of bounds, in someone else's barrio.

"What's your reason for it?"

"I don't know, I really don't like to have enemies. I stick up for my barrio and I guess for yours, too. One thing, I don't like for anyone to spit on my corner, man. But the other thing with me is that I like to be where there is a danger of getting my butt kicked, then see if I can talk my way out of it and get an invitation to return. I guess it's my way of playing 'Russian Roulette.'"

He noted that I didn't always win.

I rubbed my nose and cheek. "Yeah, I'm hep to that," I exclaimed.

David got out after a week. The system people kept their word, whoever they were. I picked him up at the front of the County Jail, which is located on the corner of Broadway and Temple Streets. I had saved up some money and through my father had bought a '34 Chevy convertible. It wasn't all that good, but it beat the Model A and its constantly flat tires. The

Chevy really had been a junk heap with a good engine. But with a blue paint job and a new canvas top and seat covers, it looked good enough. For the big event, I put down the top. I wanted to impress David. I waited for his reaction. For now, none was coming.

"Hey, little brother, make a U-turn and go down Broadway, at least to Seventh Street, okay?" I just want to see the honeys and the city before we head back across town. While you're at it, stop at a store too," he said.

I did as he directed, made the U-turn, headed south on Broadway and stopped on Third while he went into a store. He came out with a quart of milk, which he sipped while we took in the sights.

"Oh, by the way, I like your new car," he said with a wink. "I'm glad it has a back seat me and Martha can sit on when we cruise later on."

I grinned 'cause he said it had class and said, "It's about time you noticed my new car, dummy." I told him, "I'm still working at Lockheed and I got me a raise. I'm making ninety cents an hour and pretty soon I'll be making a dollar an hour. I think you probably still have your job. If you do, you'll be making a dollar an hour, for sure, since you started before me."

For now, he didn't seem concerned, so I let it all slide.

Chapter VIII

Pasterman continued having meetings with the various factions. I didn't get involved in the planning, but it was decided to have a big dance to celebrate all the truce meetings and the ending of hostilities. The dudes from First Flats would host the dance, because it would be held at Pecan Playground in their territory. All kinds of rules and regulations were enacted and the gangs promised to abide by them.

Pasterman was talking it up all the time. He felt sure that things were changing for the better among the barrios. We weren't too friendly, but at least we weren't cutting each other up. It felt good, as far as I was concerned. I didn't have to spend so much time at the corner. I could spend it with Penny. When she wasn't available, I would go off with Art and pick up on a couple of girls we had met at a dance. They were Paddies, but they really dug Chicanos.

I didn't make the dance, but I sure got the report. "There must have been twenty different barrios there, man." Butcher and Art were taking turns relating what happened. "Every barrio found a place around the wall. There were chicks from all over and, man, were they friendly. It was great, man, but you know, it was too good to last. Those guys from Mara and from Flats have been enemies for too long. I think they used the girls as an excuse to start something."

I broke in, "Well, who started it?"

Art said, "Shit, I don't know. One minute everybody is having their kicks, next minute—Pow! The war started. I thought it was never going to end."

I questioned some more. "How did you guys get out without getting hurt?"

"We just kept telling both sides we were from T-Flats and they let us slide," Butcher chimed in. "Some dudes didn't have sense enough to split and they got all busted up. They tell me when the law got there, they busted many heads. There was blood all over the place. Those poor broads. They were screaming and hollering for their boyfriends. Some guys were trying to fight with their girls hanging on to them. What fools." By the time Butcher and Art had finished their story, we had an audience.

The question around our barrio now was, Who do we support when the fighting starts again? Do we support Flats or Mara? How do we remain neutral? The guys in my barrio had friends and relatives in both areas. They tried to persuade us to join either cause. I favored neutrality. "Damn, I need a rest."

The weather fit my mood. It had been a mild winter, but now spring was making up for it. The wind was blowing. It was chilly and it kept on raining like it wasn't going to let up. "If this weather keeps up, nobody is going to be out in the streets. The dudes from my barrio won't have to choose sides. If they don't have to, then I won't have to. How cool." My personal gloom disappeared. Another thought hit my head. I'd be having another birthday soon. I would be seventeen, I could join the service and escape all this shit if I wanted to.

We found out that Pasterman had busted a leg. He had been all over the place trying to stop the beef, but only ended up getting his body damaged. He was a good man. I was sorry to hear what had happened to him. He had really worked his butt off for us and this was his reward. Besides having promoted the dance, Pasterman had also put on a talent show, which had gone very well without any negative incidents—at least I didn't see any. This was why he had been encouraged to throw a dance, though maybe he had moved too fast.

Anyway, about the talent show. What he had done was get the movie stars Anthony Quinn, Eddie Albert and his wife Margo to appear and make speeches about pride in being Chicanos and being good and all of that. After that, we had some acts, then another speech or two and a dance contest. The dance contest was won by that guy Lolo, who was at the truce meeting, and a girl named Irene, who was from First Flats. The place was full of pachucos in good spirits, well behaved and attentive. Nobody messed with anyone else's broad. I didn't bring Penny because I didn't know which way this event might go. I was sorry she didn't come and share the experience. Maybe no messing with each other's broads was why there was no trouble. I think, though, that we collectively sensed that someone really cared for us. They were attempting to reach us, so we showed respect. Respect was evident in that no one smoked dope or drank inside the place while the show was going on.

I came away feeling good that night. I talked with Pasterman for a while. Later on I thought to myself, "Gee, I know it can't happen. But if I could be anything, I would want to be a probation officer like Pasterman, because he cares and he's got balls, even if he doesn't know what the hell he's doing half the time."

I guess Pasterman knew when he was licked. He had been around us for about a year. He was steadily trying to do for us, not only in our neighborhood, but in several others. Then, after the dance and the subsequent negative results, he took a vacation. He had done some good. If he had hung around, he would have done even more. It was true that a lot of dudes were lost causes; nothing was going to reach them, but there were more of us who were looking for direction and someone or something to believe in. I found out later that he was a member of a select group within the Probation Department called Group Guidance. Their job was to reach us and help us, but they didn't let us help ourselves nor give us the time in which to do it. I wonder what part Pasterman would have played in the so called "Zoot Suit Riots" if he would have hung around a while longer.

Chapter IX

For a long time now we had been picking up in the barrio that whenever guys went downtown alone or in small groups they would end up in fights with servicemen. Generally, the guys would end up getting beaten up while the cops and by-standers watched. The cops would then bust the guys on any phony charge. All the papers carried graphic illustrations and stories of how our American heroes in uniform were kicking ass and getting us pachucos in line. All this time the fights had been confined to downtown Los Angeles. They hadn't yet gone into the barrios.

I had my own experience, which kept me out of downtown Los Angeles for a long time. Art and I had decided to go downtown after work to buy some khaki pants to wear to work. There was an Army and Navy Store on Seventh and Main where we went to do our shopping. We got bumped around by servicemen and treated poorly by the salesman, but we figured this was because we were Mexicans and it was usual for them to be discourteous, especially when business was good.

We made our purchases, then started walking down Main Street towards Third Street. We figured on getting the "F" car on the corner. Art said "Hey, *ese*, look behind us." I looked and noticed soldiers and sailors who seemed to be trailing us. We both wondered what was happening. They got closer to us and started calling us greasers, pachucos and punk Mexicans. We couldn't figure them out, but we didn't get tough either. We just kept walking. At the corner a cop stopped us and asked us what our business was. We told him we were going to get the "F" car and go home. About that time the "B" car was passing. He hollered at us to run and jump on the back end. We didn't question him. We ran and jumped on board. The cop stopped those servicemen from following us.

That night and for the next six days, all hell broke loose. Servicemen acted like vigilantes. They would roam up and down Spring, Main, Broadway and Hill Streets. In the beginning, they jumped any young person who looked Mexican or Black and dressed in drapes. Later, they went after anyone that was brown or black. White America cheered and the police stood by and watched the action. The servicemen got real brave, they got into taxi cabs and drove around barrios like Alpine, Temple, Califa and Macy, looking for pachucos. Man, they spit on our corners! They went into movie theaters, jumped guys, beat them up and ripped their clothes off. They were treated like heroes by the Paddys. All of this was reported in those two rags, the *Times* and the *Herald Express*. They wrote some inflammatory stories about how the Zoot Suit hoodlums were going to bc cleaned out by servicemen and good riddance and all that shit!

The *Daily News* was more sensitive about its reporting. I'm glad I read that paper. That way I had a better feeling, because I was hating everything that stood for "good white folks."

As I said before, the Zoot Suit Riots lasted for a week. During that time, caravans of taxi cabs went into nearly all the barrios in Los Angeles County from Watts to Pacoima. They were loaded with servicemen fresh out of bootcamp and basic training. They had been conditioned to hate, fight and kill. This was a battleground for them, a place to test their skills against a helpless people. The Mexican papers carried stories of outrage, but they were laughed at. The Los Angeles City Council passed an ordinance outlawing zoot suits.

"Kill them all, deport them to Mexico! Put 'em in jail! They're un-American! If they want to fight, why don't they join the Army?" What the hell did they think Mexicans were doing? While Anglos were waiting to be drafted, Mexicans were enlisting.

About the time the Zoot Suit Riots were taking place and we were gaining notoriety throughout the country by way of *Life* magazine and newspapers, the first Congressional Medal of Honor was being conferred to a Mexican-American for heroism in battle in Alaska. Very few people picked up on this. Damn! I was feeling bad.

In my barrio the dudes talked about a big meeting that

was going to take place on Lorena and Brooklyn in the little park. All the barrios were going to get together to see if we wanted to fight back. One night, the meeting finally took place; there were hundreds of guys there. Nobody talked about their personal fights, because everyone had read the paper or had been victims of the servicemen and their American justice. Some black dudes had come in from Watts. They said they had some submachine guns and they were ready, willing and able to fight and lend the fire power too. It was exciting as hell out there.

The plan was to begin on Temple and Main Streets and march down the street shooting every serviceman in sight. Everybody hollered yeah! yeah! yeah! I kept waiting for the law to show up.

After a while, I edged my way out of the crowd and went back with some of the guys to the neighborhood. We sat around under the Fourth Street bridge, talking about the night's events. The consensus was that we had no stomach for murder. The way those guys were talking scared the hell out of us. We talked, but I felt scared. It was okay to fight your own kind, you understood that, but murder—even if you hated those people and what they were doing to you—was a little too much. I personally decided I wouldn't go on that walk. Later, I would be glad to hear that walk never took place.

A bunch of us met the next day at the courts where some of the guys lived. Art, Butcher and Johnny had been chased by some sailors who had come over in taxis and gotten off on Fourth and Fresno. They were mad. "Shit," Eddie said, "we ought to be able to do something about it in our own barrio. The guys are fighting back in Flats and Alpine. The guys in Watts are rocking the Red car when it passes through and daring the servicemen to get off and fight. We got to take care of our honor. Well, cut the crap and let's get a plan together."

It was decided that, on that night, three guys would sit on the street car bench in front of Lasky's Drugstore, acting as decoys. They would be all draped out, so nobody would mistake them for squares. We set things up that night and it went off just as we planned. Those fools came five in a taxi and they cruised to a stop. The three guys hollered swear words at the three guys on the bench. It felt sweet. I figured that the damn taxi drivers were more to blame then anyone. They were making money headhunting.

I hollered at some of the guys as I ran to the taxi, "Help me get these Paddies." I caught the cab driver and hit him with a bicycle chain. The guys knocked in his windows, broke his headlights and put big dents in his car body. He managed to break away from me. I was trying so hard to do him in that I kept missing him and when I did land one, he kept catching it on his arm. He was screaming all the while, "Why me, I'm not looking for trouble," and I kept calling him a chicken-shit and anything else I could think of. He got away from me, managed to crawl into his car, put it in gear and split.

By the time we got back to the original targets, they had had their fill. Stupid suckers, they had been rained on with bottles and rocks, kicked, punched and knocked all over the block. They came looking to kick ass and got theirs kicked. They separated and split in different directions with guys screeching after them. I wondered if they got purple hearts for wounds inflicted during the battle of Tortilla Flats. I wondered how they told their story to their buddies.

In about an hour we were all in the garage in the back of the courts. We could hear police sirens, and we guessed that the corner was hotter than that hell I had heard about when I used to go to church. Talk about satisfaction! We drank some Dago Red, I opened quarts of beer with my molar and we toasted each other. Wow, we had kicked the shit out of the Army, Navy and Marines. How sweet it was!

The guys talked about their individual deeds. I crowed about getting the real villain. We did all this in the dark. No use letting the fuzz know where we were. Only a candle flickered as we talked, and we talked late into the night.

Chapter X

I was washing, getting ready to eat and go to work, when there was a knock at the door. My mother opened the door. A couple of white men in business suits stood there. They asked her if I lived there and could they come in and talk to me. She asked them who they were as they brushed past her to get me. They told her they were police and flashed badges. They asked me if I was Mike.

I said, "Yes."

They told me to come along with them.

I asked, "What do you want me for?"

They said, "Attempted murder."

I started to laugh. "I don't remember trying to kill anyone lately."

My mother started to cry. She put her hand on one of the cop's arms, asking him to explain what it was all about.

He was rude, but that's the way they all are. He told her, "He's going to Hollenbeck, and if he isn't released, he'll be sent to Juvie. You can see him there and get the details."

The other cop said, "You come along, pachuco. We're tired of waiting. Move, before I put my boot up your ass."

I never got a chance to eat breakfast. I told my mother in Spanish, "Don't worry, I haven't tried to kill anyone. Call my job. Tell them I'll be late or I won't be in until tomorrow."

When we got to Hollenbeck, they put me in a little room with some benches around the wall. A couple of cops whom I had seen cruising around the neighborhood finally came to see me. The interrogation went something like this:

"You from T-Flats?"

"Yes, sir."

This fat ass, bad-breath cop stuck his face into mine. He thought I was lying, 'cause I couldn't look him in the eye. It was his foul smell that made me turn my head. "Who do you hang around with? Do you know why you're here?"

"Yeah, the cops that brought me told me it was for attempted murder."

"You're right, that's why you're here. You think you're bad, don't you?"

"No, sir."

"Why did you try to kill that guy? He didn't do anything to you."

"What guy?"

"Who was in it with you?"

"Who was in it with me? In what?"

"Look, you, we already have some of your boys in custody and they all fingered you."

"I don't have any boys, but my friends wouldn't finger me for something I know nothing about."

"How about jumping that taxi driver and those servicemen?"

He shoved that one in quickly and caught me off guard. I knew the guys wouldn't cop out. They probably started with members of T-Flats—I got a flash. Taking us in last year and mugging us had paid off for them, just like they said it would.

"Do you want to make a statement? If you do, it will go easier on you, especially if you tell me who was involved. We'll treat you good."

I laughed at him ruefully. I might tell my involvement, but I wouldn't take any of my partners with me. At this point, I put my head down. I expected a punch or two, but I wasn't saying anything more. They shuffled their feet, but that's all. One of them called a uniform cop, who took me to a cell. The door clanged shut behind me. It was dark in there except for a light high on the ceiling. I felt alone, worried, but not fearful, a kind of contradiction of feelings, because I was optimistic. Things would even themselves out. They always seemed to. I thought of David. Now it was his turn to visit me. He better see me before he left for the Army and basic training. I thought, "I hope I'm out for his going away party."

A few hours later, the door opened. "Come along, hotshot," a voice said. I didn't say anything. They might think I was mouthing off and knock me on my butt, or else I might say something to give me away. I was silent, took directions, that's all. This cop took me to the front office, where he handed me over to another cop. He had a folder which I figured was about me. He put it down, told me to turn around and put my hands behind my back. For the first time I felt the bite of handcuffs on my wrists. I felt myself going outside of myself and looking over what was happening, like I might be watching a movie, nothing more.

"All right, sap, move out through that door. Don't say nothing. Move when I tell you, stop when I tell you and we'll get along."

I looked at his face, cleaned my face of any emotion and nodded.

Chapter XI

The trip from Hollenbeck to Juvie on Eastlake didn't take too long. Soon I was being processed by a clerk. After that they had me talk to a probation officer. He decided that I should stay with them while I waited for a predetention hearing. He acted like he cared about me. He asked me personal questions, clucked sympathetically and almost had me falling for his line. He tripped over his observations on my clothes, hair and way of walking, so I tuned him out. He took me past the reception room to another room, where he took off the cuffs. He had me wait while he gave them to the cop who had brought me. I looked around not liking the brown walls that looked back at me. He came back, told me to take off all my clothes and to put them in a canvas bag. After I had done as he directed, he told me to follow him to the next room, where they issued me some clothes. I started to put them on.

"Hey, asshole, don't put them on," he hollered. "Follow me to the showers, lather up and get all that grease off your hair."

After I had showered and put on my clothes, he took me to a counselor's office. A Mr. Johnson came in and sat down behind his desk, read off some rules and regulations and filled in the top sheet of a paper with my name and age. He explained that this would be a document on my behavior while I was in Juvie. He told me that my parents would he contacted. He explained, "You have to go to a detention hearing so that you know legally what you're being held for. Be cool and you'll get treated cool, but if you cause trouble, you'll be locked up."

So here I was sitting in the day room in Unit R in Juvie, trying to keep my ducktail in place with no pomade and wondering what would come next.

I was hungry, since I hadn't even eaten breakfast and I had

been too stubborn to ask for anything until now. I walked to the counselor's office, tapped on the window to get his attention, then said, "Hey Johnson, I'm hungry. I didn't have breakfast or lunch or even supper. How about something to eat?"

"My name is Mr. Johnson and supper has been served. No food is allowed in this room, because it breeds rats and cockroaches. I can't help you. Drink water and fill up that way."

"Your mother," I muttered, and went over and filled up on water, like he suggested. He followed me with his eyes, probably wondering what I had said, which was nothing bad, except in the way you say it. Towards late evening the guys were let out of their rooms and allowed into the day room where I was. This had been bothering me the most because I didn't know what gangsters were locked up and where they were from. I hoped at least a couple would be from my barrio. As they let themselves in, I moved towards the back of the room where I could see them as they came in, one at a time. If there was anyone coming in that I had problems with on the outside, I wanted to see him before he saw me. I recognized some of the guys, even placing their barrios. Most of them I had seen around Metro. The one that gave me a start and kind of scared me was a guy named Joe from Kern. He was big, bad and powerful. He had sat in on the truce meetings with Flats and we had met at several other happenings. A couple of the happenings were strained sessions involving words over girls. He and Johnny had faced out with guns, but lucky for them, there were guys on both sides to split even. Joe had smiled at me and at Johnny and said, "We'll get together later on," in a pleasant but meaningful voice.

I kept my eyes on him as much as possible while scanning the rest of the guys. There were about twenty that came in and eight of them were Chicanos, five were black and the rest white. The blacks mingled with the Chicanos around the radio. The whites went off to a corner. Some seemed scared and others oblivious to the rest of us.

Mr. Johnson walked into the room bellowing instructions. "Everyone will keep his hands to himself or find himself in lock-up. Sick call will be in fifteen minutes and if you answer, you better be sick or else. Some of you will be transferred to other units, so listen for your name. The radio is for everyone to listen to. The books and magazines are to be read, not to be marked or torn up. If I catch anyone lighting up a cigarette, I'll write him up and send him to lock-up. Don't nobody hassle me and I won't hassle nobody." He drew himself up to a full six feet two inches. He was skinny, but he looked tough and mean enough. He reminded me of Ichabod Crane, with his long arms, skinny fingers, long nose and thin lips, except he had some hard eyes. I found out later he had been a sergeant in the Army. He had seen lots of action and liked to talk about it.

The *raza* ended up together in one corner. I didn't go to them. I waited. I knew I was being checked out. They would get to me soon enough.

"Ese, come over here," some guys waved me over. I went over slowly. No smile, slight swagger. They had me figured for a pachuco, from a barrio. For sure I wasn't a square.

They nodded all around as I got to them. "You're Little Mike, aren't you?"

I said I was.

"You know who I am?"

"Yeah, you're Joe from Kern. We talked before. Our barrios have a beef going most of the time." I could taste the green sweat in my mouth and hoped I didn't get a twitch by my eye. Joe smiled a genuine friendly smile, put out his hand, which I shook, then he introduced me around.

Some agreed they had seen me around Metro, at the show and at the dances. Three of the eight Chicanos were not from barrios. They sat there looking from one of us to the other as we started swapping stories about our barrios and where we had been as individuals. We were careful not to embarrass one another by talking about jumping each other's boys. We talked and laughed at what got us into Juvie in the first place and what we thought might happen to us.

Since no one felt like challenging me about my barrio or me as a person, I relaxed and they did too. For that reason, Johnson didn't get any action that night.

It took me a long time to fall asleep. I had to go through all the day's events, even what brought me here. I saw my mother's face again. She had cried, asking why I had been bad. My father had stood by looking at me, there was no anger, there was no smile. He seemed to understand when I told him the truth of the matter. After all, I pointed, "You read *La Opinión* and hear the news in Spanish. Mexicans are in the service, they are hard working, pay their taxes and try to be good Americans. Their reward is an ass-kicking and humiliation by the notorious Gladiators. They came and spit on our corners. As young men, we had to try to kick their asses. The old folks bow their heads, but us young ones aren't going to take their shit, even if it means busted heads and having to go to jail. I'm not ashamed of being busted for this. I did it for my honor and your honor." I lay in bed and choked at my own dramatic way of speaking to my father, just like some of the passages he used to read to me from books when I was a little boy. I finally fell asleep.

During my stay in Juvie, I took a chance with the man who was my counselor and told him how things had come to pass as far as my bust was concerned. He glanced at my jacket (record folder) from time to time as I talked. He was the first adult person I had copped out to since the action took place. He made a few comments, mostly clucking sounds and occasionally he sucked in his breath. I figured he was interested and my long held-in story got me to saying more than I wanted. I even bragged a little more than I should. About the only thing I didn't give out was the name of the dudes involved with me.

He surprised me by being sympathetic. "There's been talk of investigating what the Army guys were doing and why the cops were letting them get away with it." He said he was going to get me the *Daily News* 'cause they ran stories that were honest. He continued, "You know, I've been reading all these stories about Zoot Suit hoodlums attacking people and raising all kinds of hell. I got to believe this shit. Now, you tell me your story and I got to start thinking that maybe you and your friends may be the victims. What I'm surprised about is that they aren't busting more pachucos in here. Look man, you behave while you're here, 'cause I'm one of the few who don't give a damn whether you're a Mexican or anything else. The rest of the counselors can give you a bad time if you step out of line. Do yourself a favor, short stuff, and you'll make it out of here without too much hassle. Stay away from your pachuco friends. They won't do you any good."

I thanked him for his concern and good words. If the counselors weren't there to help, who did I have to turn to? Well, I had made a promise to be good for my folks' sake. I would keep that promise in order not to bring any more shame on them. I got up in the morning, made my bed, waited for them to give me a broom and then a mop to use on the room. After that I went to wash up, then back to the room and waited to be called out for breakfast. Breakfast, as well as other meals, was served in another building we lived in. The counselor hollered out, "All right now, cover down, square it off, keep your mouth shut, listen for your name and sound off when you hear it!"

With all this done, we marched down the walk with two messengers (trustees) in front. When we got to the dining hall, the counselor hollered out for us to stop. He went through the instructions again. "Go in, find a place to sit, keep your hands on your laps, don't touch anything on the table and don't talk. Do you hear me?"

Once inside, the counselor closed and locked the door. He turned to us and said, "Everybody rise." We did as ordered. "Messenger, lead us in the prayer."

"Dear Lord, thank you for thy food and all our mercies sent. The food we eat, the clothes we wear, our health, our home, our friends, Amen."

"Sit down, eat and be quiet. I don't want to hear any loud chatter. You Mexicans read those signs on the wall. It says speak English only. That sign means it and so do I. If I catch you speaking Spik, I'll give you demerits."

The Chicanos turned, looked at him, then back to the food. Under our breaths a general salute to his ancestry was uttered. It was a daily ritual. Breakfast over, back to the dorm, general clean-up, questioning by counselors, chit chat with the *batos*, then marching off to what laughingly passed for school. Half of the action took place in school. The teachers were not too hep as to what the guys were doing. Cigarettes were smoked, punking dates set up and physical pressure was put on guys without friends in class. It was rumored that some of the teachers were queer and would do favors for the guys for a feel.

One afternoon I was told by my counselor that I would be going to court the next day. He had written and submitted my juvenile hall report. He said he hoped it would carry some weight. "Don't get your hopes up about anything, that way if things go bad it won't hurt so much. If things go good, you scored and I'll be happy for you. I've seen too many kids with their hopes up. They get a bad jolt, can't handle it, blow it in court and then here in Juvie. They lose out all around, 'cause the system can't be beat when you're a kid."

I had already been to predetention hearing. The judge told me what I was accused of. He felt my parents couldn't control me and since the charges were grave, assaulting someone without just cause, both the community and I would be best served if I waited court in the "Hall."

The next morning a messenger took me to the front of the court door. From there a counselor and then a bailiff took over. In due time they called my name. I went into the courtroom and found my mother, father, a judge, a probation officer and a man that I recognized as the taxi-cab driver all there. The taxi driver stared at me, trying to give me a tough guy look. He probably was trying to say to me, "I'd love to punch your head off, you goddamn pachuco." I was trying to answer him the same way, "Screw you, you chicken-shit. If you're so tough, come back to my neighborhood and I promise you seconds."

I got a very stern lecture from the judge before he decided to send me to a Probation Forestry Camp instead of the California Youth Authority. There was no way he was going to send this pachuco home on probation. I expected the worst, got only half, so I didn't fall apart.

The judge dismissed the taxi-cab driver after giving him a lecture on what he should and should not do with his time while on duty, which surprised me. By now, with the papers carrying stories about us pachucos and the anti-Mexican feeling everywhere, I felt no one would talk good about me or my kind.

The judge excused himself, but instructed the probation officer to let me visit with my folks for a while. I shook hands with my father, hugged and kissed my mother, then had the P.O. lead me away. I surprised myself because I was composed, with no remorse, no wanting to cry. I felt cool now that I knew what was going to happen and what I had to face. It reflected my Indian heritage.

Back at the dorm I went in to give my counselor the news. We kicked things around, then he turned me loose so I could share the news with the boys.

I wrote a letter to my girl Penny that night. It was full of love and sentiment about our having to be separated. In the back of my mind I had the feeling that she wouldn't wait for me. When I evaluated our love affair, it seemed all one-sided. I was the one that was all hung-up. She was always nice to me. She never refused to go out with me, but she never told me she loved me, or did she? For my part, I knew she was a virgin, without asking, so I didn't try anything.

Once I went to T.J. with the guys to mess around. T.J. is the common nickname for the border town of Tijuana, Mexico. While there I bought Penny a cross that was made of woven silver and a silver chain to match. It was the first real gift I had ever bought a chick. In giving it to her, it was like announcing my love and engagement to her. She really liked it and wore it all the time she was with me.

I could see her clearly with my eyes closed as I lay on my bed in my room. She was built cute and walked with a bounce that was a joy to behold. Lots of times I would walk behind her, holding her by the waist, just to feel the bounce as she walked. She liked my compliments, but blushed a lot because of them.

As I wrote the letter and thought of her, I hummed the tune "Pennies From Heaven." I had memorized the words and ended up by singing the song softly. That's the way I fell asleep. I wish I could say I dreamed of her, but I don't remember what I dreamed.

Chapter XII

The ride from Juvenile Hall to Camp Malibu was long, even though it was only thirty-five miles. The driver came down Ventura Boulevard, until he hit Los Virgenes Road, then he turned left onto a country road that brought us to the camp. It had been a long ride, because the man hit just about every signal and there seemed to be a signal at every corner. He cussed, but couldn't do anything about it. The three of us future camp inmates didn't mind too much. None of us were in a hurry to get anywhere. We looked out the windows of the Plymouth station wagon at the girls. The man had already warned us not to talk loud or holler at anybody or he'd report us when we got to camp.

Topo, from my barrio, and Johnson, a black dude from Jug Town, were my companions on this trip. We talked to each other about where we'd been and what we could expect when we got to camp. Having Topo with me would certainly be in my favor. He already had a reputation for being bad, so for sure there would be guys in camp that knew him. I could ride on his rep. Johnson had hung around with the *raza* for a long time, so he could make it with us without any trouble. He was now hanging around with blacks, bringing them together to make a "set" out of them. He would be handy to know if the other blacks were unfriendly.

As I thought out these things, I felt that I was being cold, but I figured that I wanted to survive and make the best of a lousy situation. I sure better know who the players were and have them next to me.

Topo had been busted for carrying a concealed weapon. What had happened was that he was coming down Fourth Street in the direction of the corner. I was driving along in the opposite direction. I saw him and made a U-turn. He was hobbling along like he was hurt.

"Hey, what happened, man?" I asked him with some concern. I figured he had been in some beef and they had dusted him. He grinned and opened the top buttons of his pants and showed me a shot gun he had shoved down one pant leg.

"Nah, nothing's wrong with me. I figure with all the shit flying, I want to have a gun handy just in case. I decided to walk. I figured this was the best way to carry this gun."

I cracked up and offered him a ride to the corner, even though I was going in the opposite direction.

"Chale, I'm gonna walk the rest of the way. I'm getting my kicks out of this. Let's see if I make it. See you soon, goon."

He walked off. I made a U-turn and cut out in the opposite direction. Needless to say, he didn't make the corner. The cops busted him before he got there. Now, here we were together.

Johnson got caught throwing rocks at the Red Street Car that was taking servicemen from San Pedro to Los Angeles. This happened during the so-called Zoot Suit Riots that they had busted me for.

When the shit flew with the servicemen, the kids, both Chicanos and blacks, lined the streets next to the street car line. When the streetcars passed or stopped, they rocked the streetcars and dared the servicemen to get out and fight. The police started catching and kicking the kids' asses, but when this didn't stop them, they started busting them. Since Johnson and I were basically busted for the same thing, we had a kinship. We shook on it.

Our driver drove his Plymouth through a rusty gate and down a dusty road. He came to a stop underneath a big oak tree next to a rustic-looking building that had seen better days. It looked like it might be an office.

Some guy in khakis came over to the car. He greeted the driver, nodded at us and told us to climb out one at a time and to march single file over to the door of the office and wait for him there without talking.

He asked the driver, "Say, Sam, how was the trip? See anything good along the way? How about these cherries, did they behave or give you a bad time?"

Sam answered, "John, the trip was good. No, I didn't see anything good or that you would be interested in and these cowboys were pretty quiet. They didn't give me no hassle, but damn, you'd think since they're in the U.S., they'd speak English instead of Mexican. Oh well, I guess it's 'cause of poor up-bringing. By the way, John, is Borden here? I want to eat some of his food before I leave."

"Yeah, Sam, he's up in the mess hall. Go check him out. See you before you leave. Oh, give me the jackets on these cherries." Sam handed over the folders that contained our records, and he split up the walk to the mess hall. John shouldered past us, went inside, then told us to come inside. As we went in, he took our handcuffs off. He sat us down and gave us the first of what were called orientation sessions.

John said, "My name is Mr. Cristos. That is the only name I answer to and I expect you to remember that." He was big, about six-feet-three-inches tall and about 280 pounds of fat, but maybe he was tough. You couldn't really tell. He said, "I'm the O.D., which stands for officer of the day. I'm assigning a counselor to each one of you and a living group, and when we get through talking, I'll send you up to get clothing and a shower. You're going to pull your own time, which averages out about thirty weeks. You work on fire breaks, cut down trees and stuff, about eight hours a day. You go to school three hours a night, Monday through Friday.

"If you behave, good things will happen to you. If you misbehave, it will cause your time to be extended. Smoking is not allowed. If you can't make it in camp, you will be shipped out to Youth Authority and that ain't no circus." He talked and read our records. I waited, but he made no comments on our busts. That's good, I thought, I didn't want to go through that story again.

Finally he got up and went over to a wall phone. He pulled the receiver, gave the handle three rings and waited. He shouted into the phone, "Send the dorm boy down here."

The dorm boy came down and took his instructions from Cristos. Cristos excused us and we followed this guy to the dorm. He sent me to a wing of the dorm which said "Cougars." That was my live-in group. Topo went to the "Bears" and Johnson to the "Beavers." We took beds. McLain, that was the dorm boy's name, gave us linen and blankets, a pillow and bed covers. He gave us each a foot-locker that was nothing more than a box with a lid on it painted yellow.

When we had made our beds he took us over to the supply room. Here another guy checked out clothes to us, blue denim pants and blue cotton shirts called "county liners." We were also given a helmet, handkerchiefs, sox, T-shirts, canteens with belts attached, a towel, high top shoes and tennis shoes.

McLain showed us how to fold the stuff and fit it in the box and how to hang the canteen and belts together with the helmet. He took us next door to the shower room. The shower boy gave us soap and told us to take our time showering, because it would be the last time this would happen.

We got through, put on camp clothes, rolled up our civilian clothes and gave them to the shower boy. When we had our first visit, our folks would take our clothes home with them.

We didn't do any of this silently. Since there were no adults near by, we talked freely and asked a lot of questions of the shower boy and the dorm boy. Their big concern was contraband. They wanted to know if we had brought in any cigarettes, pills or grass. Surprisingly, all three of us were clean. Those two dudes looked at us in disgust. I guess, as in all places, you adhere to the rules until you're comfy, then you set about bending them or breaking them, if only to show that you can't be completely bought off by the system.

Guys were going to get hurt getting caught behind contraband. But at least in this instance I wouldn't, 'cause I didn't use any of the things they wanted and I couldn't see how booze would ever show up around here.

We were told that the dorm, which was built in a T form, had six living groups. They were named after members of the Pacific Coast Conference. You know, the Washington Huskies, Washington State Cougars, Oregon Beavers, USC Trojans, California Bears and Stanford Indians. In due time we also found out that Camp Malibu had once been a CCC camp, California Conservation Corps camp, where, during the Depression, young men could enlist and come to work and live in the country and do such jobs as fighting fires, building parks and roads, and stuff like that.

After the Depression, camps like this were opened by the Probation Department to house runaways and then kids who should not be sent to reformatories, but given a chance to prove themselves in minimum security places.

We were assigned to a counselor. That's where Mr. Horvath came in. He worked at camp from Monday at 6 a.m. until the time he left on Thursday. His case load had ten members. During his shift he saw each one of us on an individual basis and sometimes as a group. He was the toughest counselor in camp, both with the youths and the adults. They said he was even tempered; yeah, always mad. There were always rumors going around about how he could change an inmate's attitude in only one counseling session, especially those guys who thought they were bad.

"Hey Mike," the Cougar boy leader called out, "Horvath's in the office and he wants to see you. Don't keep him waiting." Everyone let out a groan. This would be our first formal session. This guy would never take my father's place just now, except in one category, and that was "fear."

I made it to the office, knocked and waited to be invited in. A raspy voice said, "Come in." I did as ordered and finally got to see this bear in human clothing for the first time. He took a puff on a cigarette, looked at me through the smoke and said, "Sit down over there." I nodded and sat down. At this point I didn't know whether to shit or go blind. I didn't do either. He stood over me as he leafed through my folder.

Finally, he sat down facing me. "Mr. Cristos says he already talked to you. He gave you some do's and don'ts; you also got a chance to meet the camp lawyers." He took another heavy drag on his cigarette, exhaled smoke towards the ceiling and continued. "Mr. Cristos assigned me to be your counselor for the rest of the time you are here at Campo Tres. This means I'm stuck with you and you're stuck with me. I don't bargain with anyone, so don't go shopping around for another counselor."

I didn't yet know what he meant. Sitting down close to me, he didn't look all that big. He really wasn't. He was only five-feet-seven inches, but he weighed 225 pounds on a real compact body with a head that was about a seven-and-a-half hat size and no neck. His ears had a hint of cauliflower, like maybe he had wrestled or played football without his helmet on. There was no question about it. This was one mean "hombre." No one to get angry at you.

"All right, get up and let's go for a walk around the camp."

Before we hit the door, he put out his cigarette. I watched him and he watched me.

"You smoke?"

"No," I said. "I've tried, but they don't do anything for me, so I leave them alone."

"Well, here in camp they'll do less for you. As a matter of fact, cigarettes are considered contraband. If you're caught by me or any other staff person, you'll add time to your stay here."

We walked and he talked. "Look here, the way we're facing now, if you went down that road, you would come to the beach. If you go in the opposite direction you'll end up in Ventura. What I want to do right now is show you the buildings that make this camp and give you some pointers to help you get out of here as soon as you can."

"What do you mean? As far as I'm concerned, I'm ready already. I've been busted for over two months." I figured I might as well test him. I had to say something sometime.

We walked for a while in silence. Then, choosing to ignore my outburst, he went into a lecture that went something like this: "That's the woodshop. On your day off, I'll take you over there to see if you can't make something useful for your mother. You notice, you go into the dorm only through the front and you leave only through the front. Those exit doors at the end of the dorms are open all the time, but for emergency reasons only. You get caught going out the dorm by any door except the front and you've got trouble. What I mean is, only some clown planning AWOL would go out the wrong door.

"While we're at it, if you decide to leave prematurely, don't go off into the bushes. You'll only get lost, fall down and break a leg or get poison oak. Use the roads and decide right away where you want to go. If you decide to split, you will probably end up in Preston (reformatory) or some other ugly place, 'cause I wouldn't want to keep you even if I had that right."

He faced me, then. No smile, his face very bleak. "You didn't pick me and I didn't pick you, but I'll do my damnedest by you. In return you will be expected to play by the rules while you're here. If you don't and things get hot, I'll back

your play if you level with me. If you play games with me, I'll
jack you up. Do you understand that kind of language?"

I nodded. We continued walking.

"Over there are the truck sheds. The crews go out on those
trucks every day, except Saturday and Sunday. Soon, you too
will be out there with them. Those trucks are driven by F.O's—
that's forestry officers. There are five of them and there are five
crews. Tomorrow you go out with a crew called "3-5." The
three stands for the camp and the five stands for the cherry
and chump crew. When you been here a week or two and
if you're doing good, you'll be promoted to "3-4" and up the
line. You'll be a vet when you've been here fifteen weeks. Now
you're a cherry and nothing will change that but time.

"That's where we eat all our meals. It's called a mess hall.
You'll notice that since the war began, we have things a little
more military. It seems that things are more efficient that way,
but also a lot of you guys go to the service from here and it's
easier for you, because you get pre-basic training here. At least
you'll get toughened up and learn how to take orders."

"What about you, Mr. Horvath," I asked, "are you going
to enlist or wait to be drafted?"

"Man, I'm already out. I enlisted while I was still in college
and I'm out already. It was a hell of a war while I was there."
He sighed, but didn't clarify. "Getting back to the mess hall,
during your stay you'll get to work there. Don't steal any food
from the cooks and praise their cooking and you'll be okay.
Those tables and chairs over by that area are off limits, except
on visiting Sunday. Every other Sunday is visiting Sunday.
Then you and your parents get to visit in that area. The rest of
the time it's off limits. It's called 'stash valley.' Those of you
that got no sense get your parents to bring you contraband,
then you stash it there and pick it up later. Sometimes you
sneak out at night and make your pick-up. Give your heart to
your mother, because your ass belongs to me if you get caught
pulling something like that."

By now we had traveled around the camp. We went inside
the last building, which he called the recreation room. "Here
we have 'Town Hall' meetings on Saturdays after lunch. The
mayor calls the meeting to order, then he and the supervising
DPO go over the happenings in camp. If a guy is distinguish-

ing himself by being the camp cheese-eater or mess-up, his name is brought up. Fingering for the good of the camp culture is no disgrace. You learn to take responsibility for your action and the actions of your partners."

"Wow, where the hell am I. This sounds like something out of Boystown. This sucker sounds like Father Flanagan and I must remind him of Mickey Rooney. I don't know if I can handle all of this. Not with all these Chicanos in here." He was laying out principles for Paddies to live by. They certainly were foreign to this brownie.

He took me back to the office, where he lit up another cigarette, then he took me from the office to the back room. Here the "on duty" staff slept. Another door and we were in the F.O. quarters. He introduced me to Mr. Rolls, who was the chief F.O. The man was big and well built with a nice smile and a handshake that crushed the fingers of my hand together. "This cherry will be going out on "3-5" tomorrow. He's assigned to me, so I expect your men to take care of him and teach him the ropes as quick as you can, but if he's a smart-ass problem, you knock him down and let me know about it." I guess this speech was as much for Mr. Rolls as it was for me.

After school, Mr. Horvath called a meeting of the Cougars. It was held in the rec hall and conducted by Horvath and the boy leader. It was like having a club meeting or like being with the boys for the first time. Since I was part of the club agenda business, I was told the rules that the group operated by. The Cougars were still the number one group this week. The boy leader would be getting his graduation date and Horvath would put him up for mayor. As a group, they would be going to town next Tuesday to the show. I wouldn't get to go because I had to have two weeks in camp.

The boy leader made a speech to me in front of the guys. "We are the Cougars, we're number one, that's why we have most of the guys on the merit list and all the vets on "3-1." The group won't put up with a goof-off who knocks the group down and loses its privileges. If you're a messup, we'll straighten you out right away."

They were all looking at me, telling me with their eyes that they backed up his play. I wondered how Horvath had been able to get them to talk and act like this. I wondered if they

were just putting on an act 'cause the "old man" was here.
I could understand the white guys and even the black guys,
but some of the Chicanos were from barrios and never lived
anywhere else. I'd lived outside the barrio, so I could fall in if
I wanted to. I wanted to believe, but I'd been an outlaw too
long. I wasn't trusting anybody, even though I didn't want any
trouble. I left the group rather confused by all this.

We were in bed and lights out by nine o'clock. A dorm
man was at the control center, playing disc jockey until the
night man came on at ten o'clock. His spiel was simple. "The
lights are out. The talking is out. If you want to use the head,
you stop here first. If you got to pull your pud, you leave
your neighbor's socks alone. I better not see any smoke or
little lights. If I do, I'll call up your boy leader. If I'm not
satisfied with his answer, you might have a new boy leader in
the morning. Now, if you get restless or noisy, I will stop the
record playing. I leave it all up to you."

The boy leaders from the Beavers and the Bears got up and
patrolled their floor, quieting their guys down. Finally by 9:30
or so, things were placid. By 10:00 when Mr. Rodriguez, the
night man, came on, things were very quiet. They weren't
restless that night. The guys had worked hard and needed
sleep because tomorrow was another work day.

I recapped the day's adventure. I wanted to stamp it in my
mind for comparison's sake when I finally left here. No matter
how great it might be here, I was still going to leave a piece
of me here that might have been more productive somewhere
else. I had talked with Topo and Johnson only briefly. We had
waved and said little, since we were all busy trying to pick up
on what was happening. Someday we would graduate and end
up drinking lots of beer behind our adventures here.

I decided to pray, but I did so silently with my hands clasped
in front of my chest. When I finished, I hadn't yet felt like going off to sleep, so I focused in on prime people. I conjured up
pictures of my mother and father at home, then the corner and
some of the guys standing around Lasky's eating polly seeds.
Penny's face came floating into the picture. She had been writing regularly and they were love letters! I still got butterflies in
my stomach whenever I thought of her or whenever I read her
letters. Sometimes her place was taken by Carmen. This chick

had, for some reason, taken a liking to me. I put her face and figure in front of Penny. There was no use dying hard over Penny, if Carmen was there ready and willing. "Well, I'm getting tired so I can sleep. I want to sleep so I can dream, I want to dream so I can dream of you." Those were the words to a song. I let sleep, dreams and fantasies take over.

Chapter XIII

The P.O. slid in behind the mayor and we rolled out of camp towards the mountains. We drove along talking quietly. The mayor told us we were going to a fire road. From there we were going to work on some fire-breaks.

In due time we stopped, unloaded and headed for a fire-break. We were given shovels, Mattocks and McClouds. We were to clear the fire-breaks of weeds and tree stumps.

The P.O. sat on a rock watching us work. Mr. Walker, the F.O., came among us giving instructions on the use of tools. The cab boy sharpened tools and cleaned the truck, keeping within earshot of the two-way radio that might crackle and let us know that we should roll to a fire. The mayor helped the F.O. Some of the cherries got to use the word for the first time. "Let me hang it over, Mr. Walker."

"Okay, hang it over and get back here."

"Can I use the bushes, Mr. Walker?"

"Yeah, but take your tool and stomp around. You don't want no snake biting your ass."

In the middle of the afternoon, we took a break. Since it was summer, we were told we were on "stand by." This meant that we might get a call to go fight a fire. Collectively, we hoped this would happen, 'cause our collective backs, arms and thighs were hurting from this work. The vets laughed at us. "This only gets worse. You cherries are getting it easy today."

Topo was hot, tired and hostile. He looked at the guy who had talked and snarled, "You asshole. The next time you or anyone else calls me a cherry, I'm gonna jam his ass." The guy tried to chest out, but thought better of it. Johnson moved up quickly beside Topo. I just stood there. The rest of the *raza* looked around to see who else might take up for the guy who had talked. He was a Paddy and of the crew of fifteen, ten of them were Paddies, besides the F.O. and the P.O.

The mayor came up fast, got in front of the Paddy, telling him to back off. He was a ding without too much sense, but in this case, he felt the danger and moved back.

Now the P.O. and the F.O. were there too. They took Topo aside while the mayor put us all back to work again.

The day was finally over. We loaded up and made it back to camp in silence. The Paddies stared coldly at the four Chicanos and the one black dude. We were outnumbered, but cohesive. We could take them if we had to. At least I thought we could. I didn't know yet that Paddies could be tough, too.

We showered, got dressed in clean clothes and waited on our beds for chow call. They let us visit, so Topo, Johnson and I got together. Topo's mood hadn't changed too much, even though Walker and the P.O. didn't give him a failing conduct. They let him slide because he was new.

Topo was saying, "Look, man, there's about eighty guys here. About twenty Chicanos are from barrios, so they got balls. The Negroes aren't going to side with the Gringos, so that gives us about thirty guys on our side. The way them Gringos looked at us, you can believe they're willing to kick our asses if we let them. Personally, I'm not going to take their shit, even if they send me to Preston."

I must have had a face that said, "Please give me a break," 'cause Topo said, "Look, short stuff, I'm not asking you to go all the way with me. I'm just telling you I'm hot and I'm going to break a head or two before my trip here is over."

Suddenly, he started laughing kind of wild-like. This was no fun laugh. I'd heard him laugh like this before he put it on with someone. Johnson looked at him and then at me.

I was glad they called us to fall out for supper at that time. I split back to the Cougars.

We went through supper, which was really good. Borden was a fine cook. If we ever had to judge this camp on food, it would rate *número uno*.

Back at the dorm we were put on quiet. We were allowed use of the head, but first we had to get permission and only ten of us were allowed in at any give time. I was able to get over my self-imposed constipation by learning how to take a crap in the presence of others. It was simple really. You just kept your pants up over your privates so as not to offend the pilot sitting next to you. Every time you dumped, you flushed the toilet. I think this inconvenience was what was going to keep me out of the bucket from now on. Imagine going to the toilet only with permission, and then having them watch you through a window while you tried to do your daily duty.

"Hey, *cabrón*, put your cock thoughts down and get up. We're going to school now." This was the boy leader hollering at me.

Mr. Fisher, the camp school principal, also doubled as our teacher. He tested Topo, Johnson and me. He found all three of us literate. I was the most advanced, so he asked me my preferences.

I said, "I like to read novels and the newspaper. I could use some math, even if I don't like it too much, some writing so I won't forget how, and the opportunity to do some art work."

He beamed at all this, 'cause he didn't have too many students with these types of preferences and ability.

Johnson said, "I want to draw pictures, read a little bit and be left alone."

Topo surprised me, because on the outside he never went to school or talked heavy about anything that I could remember. I heard him saying, "I want to read novels and books on philosophy."

Mr. Fisher looked at this obvious pachuco with the scarred, square face and jutting jaw, bristling hair and heavy eyebrows and figured Topo was trying to jive him.

Topo's eyes began to twinkle, a new expression I had not seen there before. Mr. Fisher asked Topo if Aristotle was smarter than Socrates.

"I think Aristotle was. At least he wasn't as hen-pecked as Socrates."

Fisher was convinced and the rest of us almost fell out. Topo, the bad-ass mother, had another side to him.

Mr. Fisher had warned his class that he wanted no horseplay. If there was any, he would call in a counselor and get rid of the troublemakers. He worked with us as individuals and in small groups. Mostly he sat at his desk working on his homework from his day-teaching job. The guys contented themselves by talking quietly in the small groups. As an individual, any pachuco might have his pencil out drawing pictures of barrio life or putting his initials on every page of every book he could get his hands on. When this was done, he did the same to the desk top and chairs. The Paddies and black dudes weren't into graffitti, but they might draw cartoons and write "Kilroy was here."

We finished school and were dismissed to our dorms. In the dorm we followed the ritual of the night before. I hurried through my toiletries and went to bed. I was really tired, even though it was only nine o'clock. I didn't attempt any conversation with my neighbors on either side, so I could get to sleep as soon as possible. I clasped my hands together, said my prayers to myself, made the sign of the cross, asked God to take care of my people, then went into my routine of late, conjuring up the principals in my life.

o o o

Today was visiting Sunday and the vets were making the most of it. The cherries, that was us, looked at them with envy. We stayed away from them because the envy might turn to hostility and then blows.

While visiting took place in "Stash Valley," the rest of us were allowed in the dorm, the rec hall or the steps of the dorm.

Johnson, Topo and I sat on the stairs of the dorm, watching the cars drive up with the visiting relatives. The mothers spread picnic lunches while the fathers went to the office, identified themselves and asked for their sons.

Baldwin, another black dude, came and sat with us. He was not only a cherry but already judged a ding. He debuted in camp by hitting some guy on the head with a weight, because he had laughed at Baldwin for being skinny and trying to lift weights. He was given a break and allowed to stay in camp. He was small, skinny and mean. "The best thing about visiting Sundays is sitting here watching the sisters of the dudes. I watch them all, then I pick one for myself and at night I dream about her. It never fails, I wake up all wet. Funny how I can have a wet dream and I can plan it." He was talking to no one and all of us at the same time. He was expressing our sentiments. Most of those girls were looking good and they knew it. I sure as hell wouldn't be prejudiced at this point. Any one of them would have been good enough for me.

Topo started talking crazy again. I guess this looking and not touching was getting to him. I figured that before the day was over, he would be punching somebody out. I felt the same pissed off feeling he was expressing. Looking at Johnson and Baldwin, I guessed they were in the same mood. What could we put into words? Could we say that we were homesick, that it was unfair not to have visits, that we were tired of being bossed, that we had just gotten here and had a long way to go, that we hated everything and everybody, including ourselves, for being here?

Yeah, we were getting quietly hysterical. But so was the rest of the camp. The counselors weren't dumb, they could smell something. They were walking around among the guys, making sure they weren't grouping. But the danger was only from about twenty guys. What could they do. That question would be answered before the day or night was over.

With visiting Sunday over and all the visitors gone, the counselors breathed a sigh of relief. They breathed too soon. One Paddy kid named Detrick walked up the steps where we were sitting. Topo got up and hit him up for some of his goodies. Detrick had no sense. He said "fuck you" to Topo and kept on going. Topo hit him on the back of the head, knocking him forward and spilling his goodies. Detrick didn't wise up. He charged at Topo, screaming at him, "You fucken Mexican, I'll kick your ass for you." Baldwin hit him on the side and Topo hit him right on the mouth, splitting his lips and knocking out some front teeth. He fell on his stomach and Topo kicked his head.

Some of the Paddies from our crew came running to the rescue. I kicked one in the stomach, then hit him in the face as he doubled over. What a drag, I thought, I liked this guy. I stood over him laughing, then I was flat on my ass. Somebody knocked me down with a punch to the head that left me dizzy. I sat there wondering what had happened. I looked up at all the kicking and punching going on. Next thing I knew, someone had grabbed me by the arm and sent me flying in the general direction of the office.

"Move clown," he said, "before I kick your ass. And don't

stop until you get to the office. The rest of you, if you want the same kind of treatment, stay out here. If you're bystanding, get your butts in the dorm and on your beds. If you're not on your beds in ten minutes, you'll be on your way to Juvie." They heard Horvath, all right, and most of them split for their beds.

Topo was tangoing with two guys and Johnson was trying to cut in. I watched all this from the office steps. Some counselors tried to stop them. Horvath hollered at them to "let them go at it. Let them get it out of their system." They did as they were told, heading instead for the dorm. You could hear them hollering, "Everybody get your asses on your beds and stay there, 'cause when all this is over, you're going to pay the price."

Topo and Johnson went toe to toe with those three Paddies. I mean it was one hell of a fight. They were not talking anymore, just fighting. Whenever anyone connected with a face, you could hear the "whap" loud and clear.

It seemed like they went on for days. Nobody who got knocked down stayed down and nobody gave up. Funny thing, no one looked for weapons. It didn't enter my head to run over and help out my *camarada*. Somehow I was just another member of the audience.

I guess the beef lasted as long as it did because the guys involved were in good shape, there was plenty of room to maneuver, they had accumulated anger and they were just plain tough *batos*.

"All right, you gladiators, you made your point. You're tough, all of you. Now knock it off. If you don't stop now, when you're ready, don't say a damn thing, just go in the dorm, pick up your bedroll and bring it to the office, because you're going down. Do you hear me?" Horvath bellowed.

They knocked off punching each other reluctantly. All five headed slowly for the dorm with their clothes torn and dirty, their faces and knuckles bloody. Man, those were some blows. Those Paddies were tough, but so were Topo and Johnson. I saw them walk into the dorm, but couldn't hear anything after that.

As soon as Horvath settled the business up in the dorm, he'd be coming after me. How should I face up to him? What should I say?

Mr. Sobel walked in first. I felt a little better. Maybe Horvath would cool it in front of my group sponsor. "Well, Mike, you been getting ready for it all week. For a while there I thought maybe you had enough sense to make it through camp. I was wrong again." He sighed and lit his pipe. I figured I wasn't going to get any help here, so I didn't offer anything. "Horvath sent me down to baby-sit you, because he's going to be busy up in the dorm for a while. You want to tell me what happened?"

"Look, Mr. Sobel, I'm going to tell you my part of the happenings, but I'm not going to say anything about the other guys. I'm not a snitch, even if it means you have to send me down." I didn't look at him. I was sitting in a chair looking at a space on the floor between my legs. If I looked up, I wouldn't be able to concentrate on my replies to his questions. I wasn't going to lie, but I wasn't going to say more than I had to. If I motor-mouthed, I might say something against the other *batos*. That wouldn't do. I wasn't a cheese-eater, not even now when the shit was down.

I calmed myself down by figuring that only two things could happen. One, I would be sent down for my part in the beef, and two, I would be allowed to stay. The rest would be extra stuff. Having resolved this, I looked up at Sobel. He questioned, I answered. During our talk his pipe kept going out or else he would stop to fill it with tobacco, light it, then go on with his end of the conversation. I couldn't figure out if this was his way or if he was attempting to psych me out. I finally decided that it was just his way. I'd watched him during group meetings and when he talked to Horvath, Wells, Cristos or the campers, it was always the same. He was probably studying to be a lawyer. He questioned and then kind of cross examined, then leaned back and seemed to drink in what was told to him. Having assessed the conversation, he was ready with a verdict.

In my case, this is what happened. When Horvath finally came down to the office, he asked Sobel if he had talked to me and reached a decision. Sobel told him he had, then turned and glared at me.

"All right, stupid, get your ass back up to the dorm and on

your bed. Don't talk to anyone. Do you hear me?"

I told him I heard him good, and I walked out of the office and up to the dorm. I checked in with Mr. Cristos, who was working the control center. I asked to use the head, finished there, and went to lay on my bed.

I noticed the Cougar boy leader staring at me like he wanted to say something and knew he couldn't 'cause the whole dorm was on quiet. Then it hit me. Maybe it would be better to get sent down to Juvie. If they gave me a break and let me stay here, I would be off the merit list and on the Cougars' shit list. I would stay on "3-5," be considered a ding and be "shined on" by the Cougars, 'cause I caused them to lose first place and they wouldn't be going to town this coming Tuesday. On top of that, I might not get visiting privileges. "Damn, send me down. I don't want to put up with any more of this shit," I screamed silently.

I jumped off my bed and stalked over to the control center. Cristos told me, "Go back to your bed. The staff is making an investigation of the incident. When they're satisfied, they'll be calling all the participants in one at a time. They'll make individual decisions. But you can believe me, we're pissed off because this camp is known for being tops and a few of you assholes have blown all that. You're lucky you broke it up when we told you to. If you hadn't, we would have called it a riot and called in the sheriff. If that happened, you'd be in the County Jail by now. I've talked too much to you already, so get your ass back to your bed, you dumb ding."

The guys that participated in the fight were called down to the office one at a time. There were ten who actually got into it. The investigation went on most of the night.

Since Sobel had already talked to me, I didn't have to go down again. There was no music this night. The boy leaders watched their groups for quiet. The head was used, but only two at a time. The lights went out on time with the admonishment that if there was any talk, the lights would be turned on and the talkers would be sent down to the office. "Talk about hard times!"

Chapter XIV

The next morning, the crews rolled out of camp without us ten participants. We were sent back up to the dorm under the watchful eye of Mr. Miles, who had come on duty this a.m. to find three of his caseload in trouble. This was not a happy Mr. Miles watching over us.

For my part, I looked over at Topo and wondered what he thought of me for not following through and backing his play. He gave me the *firme* sign, which meant things were okay between us. I looked over to Baldwin and Johnson. They nodded. No problem there either. They were wearing their black eyes and split lips proudly. My lip had fattened up on the outside and was sore on the inside.

The phone rang and the expected news came. Mr. Miles hollered out and Topo was told to get his footlocker and bedroll and take it down.

Topo got his stuff together. I asked Miles if I could help. He said no. "Stay on your bed, he don't need no help." I shrugged and sat down.

Topo got as far as the door, said goodbye to me and Johnson and Baldwin, then said, "Screw this place and everyone in it. It's for jerks. I'm glad I won't be here much longer. Mike, I'll see you on the outs."

I said, "Yeah, man, be cool, walk on the sunny side of the street." He laughed and walked on down.

After a while he came out of the office in handcuffs. Mr. Rodriguez drove off with him back to Juvie and a reroute to Preston. I wondered if I shouldn't have gone off with him. I was getting a jacket with the Cougars as a ding, but it would hurt me more in the barrio with my *batos* if Topo didn't like the way I acted in this action. I also had to worry about Baldwin and Johnson. We had gotten pretty tight in the past weeks.

They had to have a good feeling about me because, as a Chicano, they had to believe we didn't hen house out on a beef or a friend, regardless of the consecuences. If they put a jacket on me in camp with the rest of the guys, I'd have to fight everyone if I wanted to stay and graduate. But if I fought, I'd be out on my ass in a big hurry. Sobel and Horvath weren't about to give me too much slack, even if they liked me or felt I could be helped. This camp was run for the good of the individual, but it considered the greater good of the group.

Hey, was that me thinking like this? What a tug of war for my emotions. I worry about my reputation with the *batos* and at the same time I want to do the right thing by the camp program. I hadn't cared about anything but my barrio and the *batos* for so long that I had forgotten that I used to be a good, clean-cut kid once upon a time.

The saying is, "You can take the boy out of the barrio, but you can't take the barrio out of the boy." This was so in my case. Hell, why couldn't I be both? Who would get hurt? I didn't want to be bad or hurt others, but I didn't want any change in my lifestyle. Being from a barrio was my thing. I did what came naturally.

o   o   o

The letters started coming in at last. This helped to ease off some of the tension. I wasn't as up-tight, because now I could compare letters with other guys. I got more addresses of guys and girls and, so as I wrote, I received answers. The letters from the girls were the ones I liked best, 'cause these I could brag on. Helen wrote with all kinds of love. The envelope smelled of perfume. She sent pictures. She was blond and blue eyed, dressed in Chicana dress, and looked good. Penny sent a picture showing her from her chest up. She was smiling as if she were thinking of me. It made my heart beat hard. Let's face it, she was the one—probably because I wasn't the one. I wondered what I could do to get her to go just for me.

o   o   o

I got a report that this guy Ronnie was going to marry Maria. That was news, 'cause I always thought that Maria was strictly for Eddie, but Eddie wasn't ready for Maria. Ronnie was a fine guy. He was from Clover and came over to the neighborhood regularly with his guys. I guess he was hanging around with our guys and making it with Maria at the same time.

Well, never mind how it happened. It seemed that it was going to be the high point of T-Flats society and activity. The way I saw it in my mind's eye, there would be a big church wedding with about ten bridesmaids and ushers, plus a best man and maid of honor and a little boy and girl as ring bearers. They would get in a car chauffeured by one of the guys. They would lead a parade of maybe ten or eleven cars, driving all over the place, honking their horns and waving at people who would be staring at them and hollering, "Suckers, you'll be sorry," while others might cross themselves and say, "Best wishes."

Every car would have some beer or wine or whiskey in it. Maybe Ronnie and Maria would drink some champagne, but they wouldn't drink too much, 'cause they would want to be ready for later. They would drive around T-Flats and East Los Angeles, then go over to Lincoln Heights and cruise around Clover. From there the caravan would head for the photo studio. There would be all kinds of pictures taken. Ronnie would have to pick up the tab for these, and when they were developed, a framed picture of the wedding party would go to each of the members of the wedding party.

From the photo studio the caravan would continue over to Maria's house, where there would be a reception. The reception was held at the bride's home to present the bride to the old-timers in the two families. This was the good part, because there was always *gallina en mole, sopa de arroz, frijoles, ensalada, tortillas* and lots of beer and wine. There would also be music. A mariachi group would be playing and the old timers would be dancing to the music, which would be loud and cheerful. The children would be chasing each other.

Behind all this screen, the bridesmaids and ushers would be trying to make-out with one another. A lot of times they had to be careful, 'cause their girlfriend or boyfriend might be close by. The intrigue was fun, but it had been known to get out of hand and someone would end up on the sidewalk with a swollen jaw and hurt feelings. A lot of times that's how you met the girl you ended up going steady with.

The day would end. There was more cruising, then everyone went home to rest in order to get ready for the dance that night. I heard that the dance was being held at the Diana Ballroom and that George Brown was going to play and Ray Vásquez was going to get to sing. The people would all be in there by nine o'clock. Then the bridal party would come in. They would march in to music loud enough to catch the eyes and ears of at least three hundred people. They would form a circle around Ronnie and Maria. They would dance to a piece like "I Love You Truly." After a while the *madrinas* and *padrinos* would join in the dance. When the piece was over, everybody would clap and cheer.

The next piece would be a fast boogie and the dance was on for sure. The bar would be open. You could buy mixed drinks or drink free beer from the one barrel that was allowed until it was empty. After that, beer was twenty-five cents a glass. There were no bottles, so that in case a fight started, they wouldn't be used as weapons.

By the time the dance was over at two o'clock in the morning, everyone would be happily loaded. They would be heading for their cars in the parking lot. Some would drive off, others would stay in their cars, drinking and making-out. A fight would break out. The guys would decide what kind it would be. Generally, they were friends fighting each other, so it would be a fair fight. They'd punch at each other, rip their shirts, bloody their noses, then sit down on the ground and drink together and crack up. If the cops didn't come, no one would leave until dawn.

And the happy newly-weds? They would go off alone to some place like T.J. or across town, where they could be alone to consummate their vows, if they hadn't done so already. As for the ushers and maids of honor, if they hit it off, they might consummate their marriage at one of the motels.

I wouldn't be home for this wedding, but I was sure that I would get blow by blow descriptions through the mail from the guys and the girls. It wasn't going to do anything for my morale.

"God, you sure are putting a lot of hurdles in my path.

What did I ever do to make you mad?" That's what I asked God during my prayers.

∘ ∘ ∘

On visiting Sunday I talked to my folks about my stay in camp. It wasn't that bad. It was good for me physically. I was walking straighter and I had put on more weight. I wasn't as wild looking as I had been. I told them about the session I had with Horvath where I blew my cool. I told them that I was feeling real good, 'cause I was half-way through the program and I hadn't gotten into too much trouble. I said that I was a vet, which meant I could work on getting a position in camp or on crew.

I explained what that meant to my father. He listened attentively. He finally said, "If you could learn the kitchen business, I could probably get you a job working in the restaurant with me." I thanked him for that. I would talk to Mr. Borden, the cook, to see if he could help out. I didn't have too much desire to work in the camp kitchen. I was getting a kick out of working in the hills and responding to fires. But it wouldn't hurt to have something to fall back on, though. A position was a position.

We finished eating and talking. All too soon visiting Sunday was over. I walked to the car with my mother while my father went to the office and checked them out. There was hugging and hand-shaking, then they were gone, leaving me somewhat empty. I shook myself loose, then went over to the office to get checked for contraband. I dropped my pants to my knees. Cristos looked. I picked them up and buckled them at the waist, then I leaned over and picked up both pant legs. Cristos checked my socks. He was satisfied. He checked my goody bag. It was full of polly seeds and Mounds candy bars. "Okay, mister, move on out to the dorm." It was times like this that I was glad I didn't smoke or use dope. I could face up to anyone clean. I could use a beer, though. One of these days I would be able to drink as much as I wanted. I cracked up to myself. I sounded like a wino. "Move over, Chonito, here I come." No, I knew I could handle booze.

∘ ∘ ∘

Some of the guys from the Cougars who had visits came over to my bed to jaw. So I sat up and we had a good session talking about our visiting experience. We got word on each other's barrios and what was happening on the outs in general. A lot of the talk had to do with the war and the fact that a lot of our older brothers and cousins were being drafted or were joining up. There were about eight of us talking it out. Some said the Marines were the best, some the Navy. Nobody said the Army. We were all talking patriotically, because we had learned something about living and working together in a cooperative spirit.

Too bad I had to come to an institution to learn about democratic principals. By golly, I was changing for a fact. But I was enjoying the change. It seemed I was loosening up. I could kid with people. I could be serious but not overly serious. I didn't swagger as much when I walked; it used to invite challenges.

The session was broken up. We were told it was time for a shower. I felt good. I whistled and sang, sometimes out loud. After the shower, we dressed, then went to supper. The good mood lasted all the rest of the evening.

o　o　o

That night I dreamed back to when I was young. You know, odds and ends, such as things which had happened to me which had me thinking I was a winner. Such as when I graduated from the Euclid Avenue School, I was voted the smartest kid, due to my perfect report cards. Then at Stevenson I made the honor rolls for the seventh and eighth grades. Then at Inglewood I continued with scholastic achievements and involvement in sports. I also became popular with both girls and boys. I had it made. I was happy and generally a pretty nice guy.

A bad taste of non-acceptance came later. When I was fourteen, we moved out of Inglewood and into West Los Angeles. I went to Los Angeles High School. I tried to fit in but couldn't. I ended up fighting because I refused to be Spanish and insisted on being Mexican and telling everybody I was. I was ignored by the kids, the teachers quit working with me, and in the gym the coaches were cold towards me. I wasn't used to this kind of treatment. It hurt me and affected my school work.

I ended up with a few good friends, but they had wayward ideas and they showed me their way. I had turned fifteen. I used the money I had saved picking apricots during the summer to buy a '34 Ford. My friends would help out by stealing gas so we could go cruising. They also brought the chicks around. I learned about passion cramps and necking while cruising around. It was kind of nice, because we ended up going steady with different girls each week, kind of passing them around among us. They didn't seem to mind that I was Chicano. On the other hand, I did have an experience that bothered me. One girl, Margie, wanted to take me home to meet her mother. One of the guys told me, "Look Mike, don't get pissed off, but Margie's mom is prejudiced, so Margie wondered if when you met her mom, you wouldn't tell her you're Chicano. If she asks, tell her you're French. Anyway, you are part French, aren't you? Margie was embarrassed to ask you herself, because she was scared to hurt your feelings."

She was right, my feelings were hurt. But what the hell, if she thought that much about me, I should be cool. "Yeah, man, I understand and I'll do what she asks. What the hell, what's the big deal in being Chicano, anyway? It sure don't get you anywhere."

"You're a good head, Mike. Don't worry, we all like you and you'll always be our friend, regardless." He made me feel good. In those days I still wasn't wearing my Chicano chip on my shoulder, daring people to knock it off.

About this time the old man came home and told us to pack up, we were moving. A few weeks later I was walking down Grande Vista to Fourth Street. This is where this barrio shit began for me.

o o o

It had been months since I had been busted. The papers had continued writing about the fighting between "pachucos" and servicemen, calling it the Zoot Suit Riots. I read that it was all a sinister plot by saboteurs to start race wars in the United States in order to weaken the people. I laughed along with a lot of other *batos*. We lived in our barrios doing things the way we saw fit. We worked a little, went to school a little, had some home life, made a little love and messed around a lot. This was our life style. We ran towards it. Who needed more?

The *Daily News* ran several stories about the war. Towards the end of the year, the U.S.A was getting its ass kicked everywhere. But even as this happened, the paper ran stories of personal bravery on the part of individuals in all parts of the world and in all branches. I looked through the stories for mention of men with Spanish surnames. I found some names in a list of several servicemen. This made me swell with pride. The main reporting was in Europe and in the South Pacific. There was still some action in North Africa.

I noticed that the paper had taken to writing a list of casualties from the Los Angeles area. I didn't recognize anybody on the list. I guess I really didn't want to.

I read where the mayor of Los Angeles and the City Council were going to outlaw "drapes" or, as they were better known, "zoot suits." They used the excuse that people who wore them were hoodlums. White America in Los Angeles was angry because the zoot suits used so much cloth. Zoot suits were un-American. That's all there was to it!

In another section of the paper, a group of people were getting together to do something about racial discrimination. They announced that the United States should have all its people united. We were locked in a death struggle with the Axis. We should stand together or we would surely fall. All the names were Anglo. I wondered where the Chicanos were. They were talking about something called human relations, that we should be considerate of one another. We should give each other a chance to understand one another. That was okay with me, but I wondered if anyone would ever come by and ask me what I felt. I doubt it. Those were big-time people.

I read the want ads. All the aircraft companies had ads for all types of people. Everything was patriotic. I wondered if they would hire guys with records. Probably not. They kept talking about how they only wanted patriotic Americans. I didn't feel I was one of those. I was a drag on society, being busted here instead of working in the industry or joining the service. I guess I just wasn't much good. I started getting down on myself, sniveling, and I didn't like it.

I turned the pages, trying to shake this bad feeling of self-worthlessness. I read the comic strips. The cartoons were okay. Gordo was driving his "comet" around, using wine instead of gas. He was a jolly fat man who shared his beans and cheese and tortillas with his friends. That included his Gringo comrades. He was a gas. Gus Arriola was a good artist and a good story teller.

Chapter XV

I got up to Camp 3-1 crew, first as a crew member and then finally as cab boy. That was a hard job because you had to believe that you were not a flunky for the crew chief or the F.O. Your job was to check the tools, keep the inventory, and make sure the tools were in good working order. Also, the truck had to be shined and kept clean. It was always full of dust at the end of the work day, so you spent much of your own time polishing it. Pride, man, pride. Camp 3-1 was and had to continue being *número uno* and you were duty bound to keep it that way. You never knew when you were going to meet up with other camp crews. You had to be *número uno*.

o   o   o

The truck radio crackled, "Camp 3-1 respond." The voice talked to Wells, giving him instructions as to where the fire was and how to get there. The crew had quit working and was waiting for commands to be issued. "Load em up, fire chief," Wells ordered. "All right, step up and load up so we can roll." The crew moved swiftly to the loading platform behind the truck. I dropped the steps and signaled to the fire chief that it was secure. I stood by while the fire chief climbed the steps, then gave the command. "All right, step off with your left foot and your tool in your right hand. When you get up, hand your tool to the truck boy." He gave these instructions coolly. He had done this before. "All right, load up."

As soon as they loaded up, Wells headed for the cab to start the truck engine. My job was to pick up the stairs and hand them to the truck boy, who then secured them by way of a lock bolt. I then took the tire chocks off and handed them up to the truck boy.

Wells gave a couple of blasts on the siren, which prompted me in the direction of the cab. I jumped in and we were off and running. Nobody had said anything, but every one of us was wired up. We really dug this action. Wells tooled the truck down the firebreak and then onto a road. When he hit the road, he told me to put on the siren. This I did. It added a touch of drama. Wow, like the Marines to the rescue. Charge! "It's a grass fire, Mike, but there's a couple of homes in the area, so we have two jobs. One is to put out the grass fire and the other to make sure those houses don't go up. On top of that, the people are still there. They think some kids playing with matches started the fire and they got scared and ran. Now they can't find the kids."

This was all shaping up like some "B" movie. Maybe the crew would end up being heroes. That was okay with me. I could just hear the radio news telling the world about how we had stopped a fire from becoming a major disaster and had saved two houses and two lost kids who, at first, were feared burned in the fire. Yeah, that all sounded good. We would get respect, people would look up to us, the other campers would be jealous, even the other camps would look up to us. "¡Viva Campo Tres! What a daydream!"

We topped a couple of rises, then we could see the smoke. A few more twists and turns and we came upon the scene. There were a couple of fire trucks already there. They were pouring water around the edges of the blaze. The other camp crews had been alerted, so they would join us soon.

The truck rolled to a stop. I jumped out of the cab, ran around to the back and the truck boy gave me the wheel chocks. I put them in place, then ran back and uncoupled the stairs. The crew stayed put. They would move out when the F.O. gave the word. Wells went over to talk to the fireman to get an idea of what was going on. I got a quick flash. It made me feel proud. Real good! Wells was so sure the crew knew what to do that he left us alone to do it. In a way, he was showing off to the firemen that he was in full control and that his crew was disciplined and could handle the action. I noticed that the fire chief also got the message.

He pointed out to the crew quietly but forcefully that they were Camp 3-1, that there was only one Camp 3-1, that there were people watching. "Stay sharp, stay clean, we're the best. You better hear me now." With this he walked down the stairs.

The F.O. high signed and the crew chief reacted. "All right, step down." The crew obeyed without a word. The truck boy handed out the tools on command of the crew chief, based on his quick assessment of what would be needed.

"On your left foot, next stop," he bellowed. He headed the crew in Wells' direction. I stayed by the truck.

The crew made it up to where Wells was busy chit-chatting with the county firemen. The fire chief stopped the crew and told it to stand by. He walked up to Wells and got his instructions. I could hear what was being said. The county firemen were drinking coffee and looking like heroes. They also looked over the crew. I bet their boss was jealous, wishing he could control his men like our F.O. had us under control.

After some conversation and arm waving, the crew was on its way. They would throw a ring of men on one side, cutting down the weeds and making a ring around the fire. At this point, the fire was burning slowly but steadily, feeding on dry autumn grass, weeds and small tree clumps. The immediate danger was a wind change.

Other crews from our camp came roaring up. Wells got together with the other F.O.'s. They decided on their strategy, then put their crews on the fire line. It was hot, heavy, laborious work, but our guys were up to it. They were in fine shape and equal to the task.

After a while, a Salvation Army truck rolled up. It had coffee and donuts for the fearless firemen. This pissed me off, because the guys from our camp were doing the work and the firemen were standing around goofing off and getting the credit and the coffee and donuts. Wells came through for us. I heard him ask for some coffee and donuts for his crew. He was told that these goodies were only for bonafide firemen. He told them to stick it, called the fire chief and told him to pull the crew out.

"If the boys aren't good enough for your coffee and donuts, they're not good enough to fight your fire," Wells stormed.

"Hey man, take it easy, you know the rules," one fireman said.

Wells ignored him, turned and said, "Chief, load up."

I dropped the stairs, the crew loaded up. I pulled up the stairs. Wells stalked up and into the cab. He started the motor, hollered for me to pull the chocks. I did as directed, handed them up to the tool boy, ran and jumped into the cab with Wells. He was swearing, at first under his breath, then out loud. I sat there admiring him, glad he was my F.O., glad I was a part of Camp 3-1. I knew that those men he was leaving behind were his drinking buddies, but his camp and crew were number one with him.

He drove the truck to another perimeter and stopped. We went through the same exercise, unloading the crew, etc. Only this time he talked with the crew for a while. "We're going to stand by here until I report our position and get instructions. One thing, we are not going to pull hose or do any work for any of them flatland jerks. Chief, check with the truck boy for sharp tools. Also, check for water in your canteens. I expect we'll have a field kitchen out here soon, because this fire will go on for at least another day. If that's true, prepare to sleep out here tonight. That's all for now, except you find the shady side of the truck and take ten until I tell you what I want next."

I checked out the cab, wiped the hood of the truck off and made sure my job had been taken care of, then I went over and sat down with the rest of the crew.

"Hey, Mike, what the hell was that all about. How come we got pulled off the line?" the chief asked. "Hey man, our F.O. is straight. What happened was that he was trying to get us set up for some coffee and donuts when we got our next break, and they told him the goodies were off limits to us. He blew his cookie, told them to jam their goodies and fire, and split on them. I guess that's what Campo Tres is all about." They nodded approval. This crew belonged to Wells after that.

We spent the rest of the night working on and off. We got some real good chow and we looked good while working. We didn't get a very good night's sleep, because we were pretty hyped up. At dawn we were relieved by another fire crew. We loaded up and headed back to camp.

When we got back to camp, we got rid of our gear, washed up and then split up to the mess hall for breakfast. Those that had not been allowed out of camp to fight the fire asked us all kinds of questions. Baldwin, who had made it to 3-1, had rubbed himself with soot from the fire and came in looking like one of those war heroes from "Back to Bataan." He gave a vivid account of the fire. "3-1 probably saved lives and property. I wouldn't be surprised if we weren't featured in the newspapers because of our outstanding exploits."

Johnson got fed up with Baldwin's account. "Shit, Baldwin, your only claim to fame is that you 'hung it over' and pissed on the fire. The fire couldn't stand the smell and surrendered. Now, shut up and let me eat."

"Aw, shut up, Johnson, you're just jealous 'cause I was looking good doing all those rescue missions and all you got to do was pull hose for your white friends on the Fire Department."

It was good natured. What was being said was that we had been there. Notch another job well done for Campo Tres.

Chapter XVI

Johnson and I were called down to the office on Friday. Our counselors wanted to talk to us. The bets were on that we would get our dates. We weren't saying anything. I was getting that fatalistic feeling, you know, think the worst. That way, if it's bad it won't hurt so much, and if it's good, well, you know the feeling will be fine.

We got to the office, looked at each other as if to say, "It's been a long time coming, baby, but now it's here." We shook hands and I knocked and asked for permission to enter. Horvath's raspy voice shouted out at us to come in. I let Johnson in first, then I walked in. Mr. Miles and Mr. Horvath seemed to be caught up in some debate. I tried to eavesdrop and not get caught at it. They were talking about Johnson and me, but I wasn't clear what the deal was.

Mr. Miles, who was Johnson's counselor, told him to accompany him to the counselling trailer. He had Johnson's folder with him. Mr. Miles was cool and he generally cracked a joke or two to put us at ease, but not this time. Horvath wasn't smiling either. He waited until Mr. Miles and Johnson had cleared out, then he started talking.

"All right, cab boy, I want you to sit down and listen to me. What I've got to say is important to your future here and when you hit the bricks, so pay attention. I'll talk and then I'll ask you questions and see what kind of answers you come up with."

He set the tone. He wasn't hostile or tough talking. It was more of a father and son talk, where the father wants to let the son know that this is a serious discussion that should not be taken lightly.

"The fact is that you have been here long enough for me to observe you on a daily basis. You have grown up mentally and filled out physically. You've fought me and I've fought you. That is natural and normal. With this in mind, I offered your name to the staff for consideration for graduation." He stopped, pulled out a cigarette, lit it, inhaled, blew out smoke and coughed. I watched, waited, died and came alive when he related that the staff had approved with very little opposition.

"A strong point in your favor is that you don't use dope and we staffers are one hundred percent against it. You don't smoke, so you never got caught with contraband, although there were plenty of times when you were suspected of doing favors for those who do. Your main deficit is that you are a damn pachuco and nothing or no one is going to shake that out of you. That's too bad, because if you could shake the *batos* loose and stand on your own two feet, you could make it by yourself. I try to understand people like you, but I can't. Maybe if I was a 'bean' and lived like you people do, I would understand. I know one thing, you people don't grow tall, but you have much soul."

During this time I would take turns looking at him dead in the eye, then shifting my eyes down, then up and around the room. "God damn, I passed for graduation and Horvath the Horrible was actually laying some praise on me and my people."

He knew I was watching him and finding him out. He toked harder on his cigarette, trying to cover up. "All right, now for a few questions. You have about five weeks before you graduate, what do you expect to do?"

"I expect to keep my nose clean, counsel with you, work hard at being cab boy and help the Cougars by keeping them in first place. I expect to talk to the new boys, especially the *locos*, to try to get them to be cool while they are here, sir."

"Look here, Cougar, you answered that like you been rehearsing what to say," and he laughed, so I laughed. I hadn't rehearsed, but I had been down the road long enough to say the right thing to any and all questions.

"What are you going to do when you get out?" he asked.

"I'm going to the Board of Education, get my transcript, and go re-enroll at Roosevelt. Oh no, I can't go there, we don't live in the district anymore. I think I have to go to Fremont. I'm going to get a work permit, too. I expect to get a job, if they don't hold my being in camp against me," I said.

"Okay, those two questions and the answers will hold me for now. I want you to stay loose as a goose, because these last few weeks will be the hardest for you to take. The guys will make demands, the staff will make demands, and your head will make demands. Just try to stay level headed and you won't blow it. You know what I'm talking about. You've seen other guys blow it. When they do, all we can conclude is that they weren't ready.

"By the way, since you're already seventeen years old, you don't have to go back to school, but I'm counting on you to do it. A little bit for me, 'cause after all, I've been your father for a while, in a manner of speaking, so I have an investment in you. But the big winner or loser is you. Check it out. You might like it."

"Oh, by the way," he finally said, "I recommended you for mayor. The staff is kind of divided on this, since you don't hold any first class positions, other than cab boy. Dominguez is graduating next week and that will leave the assistant mayor position open. You probably will get that position for a week, and then if you've done a solid job, you'll probably make mayor."

"Timber down!" I almost fell off my chair. I wanted to hug him. I wanted to cry, I wanted to get the hell out of the office and shout a great big Mexican yell. "AH-HOO-AH!"

I sat and stared at him for a while. I got up. He got up. We shook hands and I went out. He understood.

"How crazy," I could hardly wait until I got to the dorm to tell everybody. Half way up, I let out another yell. "Yaa Hoo!" I made it to the dorm and over to the Cougars, where they crowded around congratulating me.

○　　○　　○

It was time for supper, so we fell out. I went through the ritual, but with a lot more zest than I had in the past. I paid attention to detail. The Cougars were looking good and I was feeling better.

After supper, O.D. Cristos tapped for order. The graduates were presented. Their counselors made speeches on their behalf, then they were allowed to speak. I watched them closely.

I thought the two Anglos had floated through camp while the Chicano had really tried. The Anglos were going back to their neighborhoods in Compton and Long Beach. The Chicano had joined the Marines. He wasn't from any barrio, so he had nothing to go back to. He had been a damned good mayor and fire chief. He should make a good Marine. He was a leader and he was big, and when provoked, he could be an ass-kicker.

"Just think," I said to myself, "in a few weeks I'll be up there too, getting my diploma and making speeches. How fine." I finally thought of Johnson. He had come in with Mr. Miles after supper had started. I couldn't read his face. Man, I hope he didn't blow it. They turned us loose after graduation. No school tonight. They figured we needed a night off after all that fire fighting.

Johnson headed for the day room. After I saw to my Cougars, I split after him. He looked down.

"What happened, cool?" I asked.

"I don't want to talk about it," he spit out.

"That means you didn't get your date, right?" I said quietly.

"Yeah, dammit, that's what it means, it means you got yours, but I didn't." He spat that out.

I took it and sat there without saying anything.

Some of the guys came in. Louie had his guitar. He tuned it up and then we sang some songs, kind of quiet like. "Soldado Razo" was a favorite. We sang that a couple of times. It's a song about a guy who joins the Army, leaving behind his mother and girlfriend who cry over him. He promises not to return until he makes sergeant and the war is over. He asks the Virgin Mary to protect him and his loved ones. It came out real fine. We kind of imagined we were in the Army. Each one of us was the *soldado razo*.

I looked over at Johnson. His face had softened. He was ready to talk. He told me that Mr. Miles had put him up for graduation, but it had been denied. The staff felt he needed a little bit more seasoning. Johnson said he nearly blew his cookie with Mr. Miles but controlled himself, because then they would have been right. He also remembered when I pitched my bitch and what it got me.

"Man, we do live under stress for sure. To my way of thinking, Johnson, you're one of the coolest dudes in camp. Maybe there is something else happening at the pad that held the staff back."

To Johnson I laid on advice of a person secure in the knowledge that I had my date and nothing could go wrong.

"Look here, brother, by next week Mr. Miles will call you in again. This time they'll pass on you. What you got to do is show them they were wrong. Go back to your group, shape them up. Eat cheese if you have to, but remember it's for a cause. Because if you blow it, there ain't gonna be no mellow times at the ballroom," I said.

Johnson picked up and said, "I get your drift, little buddy, and you know I'll be cool and eat a ton of cheese if I have to. I want to see my little girl in the worst way. Thanks for talking, and I'm sorry I swore at you."

◦   ◦   ◦

Everything seemed okay at home, except for my brother Pablo; he was another matter. I was trying to set a good example for this guy. He looked up to me because I had a good rep among the *batos* from my neighborhood, as well as a lot of other barrios. He liked to go out and say he was my brother. He wanted to have the same reputation or an even badder one. The trouble was, I didn't consider myself especially bad or even that *loco*. He thought I was tough and he tried to live up to that reputation. He was not adverse to using a lead pipe or a knife on somebody. He didn't mind pulling a job or two and he dearly loved grass. Can you imagine? He was just turning sixteen and he was already on his way. If he lived through the gang fights I heard he'd been involved in lately, it would be a kick in the ass to see me graduating and his coming in. It was like school. I'd be leaving a school and he'd be coming in. "Well, blood, best of luck. I'll have a talk with you, but if you can't hear me talking, then shine it on."

◦   ◦   ◦

I did some mind picturing. You know, picture flashbacks. The corner was still there. I transported myself over there for the hundredth time. The wall of the malt shop had a big sign painted on it. It said simply "T-Flats." Some of the guys showed up. I had a camera, so I lined them up and took their picture. They were all young and good-looking, just like the song that Jesse Pinetop sang about our barrio. Eddie was in his sailor uniform. Butcher was home on furlough and wearing Levis instead of his sailor suit. The others in the picture were Chapa, Ballena, Joe, Rudy, Pope, Jesse, Pato and Chueco. They were just a small part of what made up the barrio of Tortilla Flats and the reason why Horvath hit the nail on the head when he agreed with me: "You can get the boy out of the barrio, but you can't get the barrio out of the boy." We attracted one another. There was a bond between us that was very strong. There probably would be several adventures with this group. Some things to laugh about and some to hang our collective heads over.

After the picture-taking, my feet took me across to Lasky's for a coke. Lasky had sold out and gone to live in the San Fernando Valley. I couldn't ever figure out whether he liked having his drugstore in our neighborhood. I know he and his wife had to put up with a lot of our bullshit, but he never got robbed and the stealing was petty.

Then I went over to talk to Blanco, the barber. He was older and the corner philosopher. He knew how to deal with us. Nobody ever thought of messing over him, because he had a story for you all the time. Next, over to the Star Market, in one door and out the other. Now over to Frank's Liquor Store. Frank was another philosopher. He was waiting for us to come of age so he could sell us liquor. For now, whenever we wanted a beer or any other type of booze, we had to depend on Abie and Chonito, the two winos, to get it for us. I zigged back across the street to Frank's Gas Station. He did a good business selling gas and repairing cars. With the freeze on new cars, people were willing to spend more money on car repairs, since they couldn't buy new ones. I always wondered if he sold black-market gas. He never sold me any. The man was careful, I guess. He probably only sold it to his older, better customers. Well, we weren't that tight with him, mostly because of his wife, who didn't like Mexicans too much, at least the pachuco variety. On the other hand, she didn't have too much to offer. She was big and fat and didn't talk English that well, 'cause she was from Russia. I wondered what she had to be prejudiced about, being that she was no winner herself.

Let's see now, what else was crowded in that half block or so of business around Fourth Street, Fresno and Grande Vista. There was the Maternidad Santiago. This lady was a registered midwife. At least that was what I was told by a few of the people who used her services. I wondered if she didn't pull off an abortion or two also. Now that was a good contact to have, 'cause you never knew when that kind of expertise might come in handy. Next to Lasky's Drugstore was the shoe repair store. The old man did a lot of business with the *batos*, because after we bought shoes at Price's in downtown Los Angeles, we had to have them altered to fit the style. This meant removing the rubber heels, replacing them with leather and then adding horse shoe tappers. After that, another sole was added, plus another tapper on the toe of the shoe. After that we had to buy dye. If the shoes were brown, they had to be dyed cordovan. If they were black, they had to be spit shined.

Across the street was the New Star Market. They had to compete with the larger, older Star Market. They sold Mexican food like *tortillas* and *menudo* on Sunday. Their main claim to fame was that the owners, Mr. and Mrs. Mendoza, had four daughters. They were nice square-looking chicks, a bit young, but pretty soon they would be old enough to think about seriously.

On the same side of the street, there was Evelina's Cafe. This was the neighborhood bar. I hadn't been able to go in there yet. Maybe by the time I got out of camp I'd look old enough to go. For now there was no attraction, because none of the gang went in there. Mostly our parents went there for drinks and none of us were interested in meeting our parents in there, least of all me. I could just see me in there with my father. He would probably kick my ass on the spot.

The rest of my time was spent meandering around the boundaries of my set. On the east it was Lorena, on the west Evergreen, on the north, First Street and on the south, Sixth Street. This was our barrio. This is what we fought for, talked about and argued about. This was our nation. We didn't let anyone spit on our corner!

○   ○   ○

Next thing I knew, it was daylight and it was time to get up. No, I wasn't at home tucked in my bed. I was in camp. I jumped out of bed and headed to the can. Wait a minute, it's Saturday, so no work. We get to sleep over another half hour, but who the hell can sleep. I did my duty, saluted the day counselor and made my bed. I dressed, then lay down and waited for the call from the day counselor to get up. I remembered that he liked to get us up with early morning jazz records, so I jumped up, went over and asked him if I could select the records this a.m. He said that I could, especially since I had lucked out and got my date. It's funny how when you're doing right, people pop up to push you along. When you're doing bad, nobody is around to give you a push in the right direction. Anyway, I pulled out some of the records that suited me. For sure we weren't going to get up listening to any cowboy tunes.

I set up a stack of 78's, starting with Hamp's "Boogie Woogie," then take the "A Train" and finishing off with "Summit Ridge Drive." All of these were lively and calculated to get the *raza* and the blacks boogieing down the aisles to the head without any trouble. The Okies in the crowd would probably moan, but what the hell, this was my show and my choices.

I made it to assistant mayor. Sobel had a meeting with us where we discussed the need for a Cougar boy leader. I was given an opportunity to at least give my views on who the boy leader should be. Sobel thanked us for our help in trying to pick our leader through the democratic process. What we, as a group, might have to say in terms of picking a successor might be taken into consideration. The final selection would be up to Sobel, because he had to have someone he could work with.

Currently, there were fourteen of us in the group. I was leaning toward a Chicano, but only because he was a Chicano. The black dude wasn't ready, but the truth was that this white dude, Frazier, was ready. I had to make a decision. I went the way of the camp and picked Frazier. There was no cheese eating here. I picked him 'cause he was ready, not because of his color or his ethnic origin. It was nice to know that when the choice was made, it was in favor of Frazier. The other guys swallowed their disappointment and said nothing. My speech to the group was that they try to maintain the tradition that was established a long time ago, that the Cougars were number one and should remain so. Frazier was red faced and really grateful to the guys and Mr. Sobel for being selected. He promised to work hard and represent the Cougars to the best of his ability.

With two weeks to go, I was called in by Mr. Horvath. This time there were other counselors there, so I knew that the meeting was to give me direction if I were to be made mayor and to hear me out. I was going in for a job interview, which would result in my terminating my past seven-and-a-half months existence on a positive note.

Let me run that one through again. I am all excited because I am going to be interviewed for the top position in the company. I am the top candidate, like all the others have been. If I get the top position and I do a good job, I will be laid off in two weeks. This is an honor for me, for my sponsor and my counselor. The honor of the top position will be duly noted in my discharge as a real accomplishment.

I knocked on the door, waited to be asked into the office, then came in when I was told to come in. They were seated around the table they generally reserved for playing poker late on weekends. This time Horvath would try to run a bluff on them by making them believe he was holding a royal flush. Well, maybe I wasn't a bluff. Maybe I was a good hand. Miles, Horvath, Sobel, F.O. Rolls, Principal Fisher and O.D. Cristos were there. Some smiled, some nodded. I stood until they told me to sit down.

Horvath opened up the session. "Mike, we won't keep you waiting and worrying about the outcome of our vote. It was unanimous that you be appointed mayor of the camp. There was some thought to keeping you longer in order to go after the governor's position, but you had too rough a start, which you probably couldn't overcome. I'm telling you this so you can get an idea of how far you've come. We hope that you appreciate what you have gained, because you were lucky enough to come here. You've cleaned your gut of hate, you can take direction, you can lead, you know you can make it 'education-wise.'"

Horvath quit talking and huffed a bit. He lit up a cigarette to cover his feelings. He was having another one of those jags. Sobel worked on his pipe and asked that I help him with the

Cougars. He brought to everyone's attention the fact that the Cougars were holding the main position. This was bragging, but it was traditional. Mr. Fisher asked me to help tutor his students. F.O. Wells reminded me that, as mayor, I would be crew leader of the truck he drove. He would give me help, but the rest was up to me. "In a way, you're going to get paid for all the off-the-wall shit you pulled when you rode my truck before. What goes around comes around." Miles didn't make any observations. He just smiled and shook my hand. O.D. Cristos cleared his throat. Everybody shuffled their feet, looked at each other and got ready for his monologue.

I fixed my eyes on him and closed my mind. I can't tell you what he rambled on about. Luckily the dorm called out that the lights were going out and they wanted a couple of staff people to prowl the area and the dorms, because it had been visiting Sunday and the natives were restless. The volunteers strode out and me with them. Cristos probably told me that the responsibility of being mayor should weigh heavily on me, that I should take the duty seriously, that he wasn't one hundred percent convinced I could do the job, but he trusted the staff's judgment. Did I hear him say this to me or had I heard him say this to others? Probably somewhere in the middle.

Chapter XVII

I wish I could say that the last two weeks of my stay at Campo Tres were quiet and uneventful. The fact is that a couple of things happened that helped pass the time and at the same time added excitement to mostly commonplace days.

It being the fire season, we made it to another fire. This one lasted for a week. I felt sorry for the guys that were graduating that weekend. The crews were out and the graduates had to work on crew until it was time to come in. Graduation didn't bring you in early from crew. I asked Dedrick, who was graduating after some forty weeks, how he felt about not leaving on time. "Well, I'll tell you true, Mr. Mayor, I been waiting all this time and now that I'm near to leaving, I really don't know where I'm going. L.A. ain't no place for this country boy. It's too fast. I really got nothing on the outs. Not even a kin in California. I'm scared to go back to Arkansas. As much as I've bullshitted myself and all of you about the outs, the only real family I've ever had was this made-up one here in camp. You know I got in trouble on purpose. I got into fights with your friends and hassled you 'cause I was scared I would get an early date. They busted me for vagrancy, not for anything high power, like you guys. Well, now you know that as far as I'm concerned, graduation day can come and go. Me, I'm scared of what to do on Saturday morning. For sure that field P.O. isn't going to bother with me until Monday, if at all."

Damn, he really had me thinking. Too bad he never opened up before. Here, most of the *batos* had been down on him because he acted like such a jerk at the wrong time. I was grateful for what I had to go back to.

"Look here, Dedrick, if you don't want to go back to Arkansas, you don't have to. But you know, L.A. ain't the only place to live. You can go live in the San Fernando Val-

ley. That's country. I bet you could get a job on a farm or
something and later, when you get off probation, you can get
in the service and build yourself up another family. Think
about it and talk it out with Miles, your counselor. I know
you got race hang-ups, 'cause you're a redneck and all that
shit, but Mr. Miles is real smart, even if he is Negro. Give
him a chance and he'll give you a chance.

"One other thing, get that stupid prejudice out of your system. It won't let you go nowhere. If you don't know what I
mean, counsel with Horvath."

He looked at me for a while, then thanked me. We never
had really liked each other. We probably wouldn't in the future, but here we were, he confiding and me giving out with
advice and me just a "Mexican," which was pretty low in his
estimation.

I don't know if he followed through on my suggestions or
not. I don't even know who came to pick him up. In fact, I
don't even know why I brought him up in the first place.

All week the crews had been jamming on fires. The staff
felt it was finally controlled and voted on a treat for all of us.

o   o   o

Friday morning all the crews went to Zuma Beach. The
cooks prepared all kinds of goodies, including watermelon and
steaks, homemade bread and the like. Before we left camp, the
staff and F.O.'s thanked us for all the work we'd put out and the
great way we had behaved as a camp. I, as mayor, was given
the opportunity to say a few words. "I'm asking that you have
a good time, cooperate and not screw things up, since we're
being allowed to mingle with the public on the beach."

The guys promised to behave. I decided to stay close to the
boys from Camp 3-5. If anything happened, it would happen
on this ding crew and I wanted to be in a position to head it
off. With only a little over a week to go, I didn't want anything
bad to happen.

It was one hell of a good outing. A real tonic for everyone.
The beach was full of civilians. We didn't eyeball anything
except the girls. But the word was out from the staff, "You
can look the girls over all you want, but keep your mouths
shut and your hands to yourselves. Smoke if you got them,

get caught smoking and you'll see some extra time tacked on. Now that we got that out of the way, let's go have some fun."

Things were going great, I mean really. Then the damn phone rang and we were off and running. Wells got on the horn, "All camp crews get rolling." What a spectacle. We grabbed for our gear and split for our trucks double time. I saw one guy grab a watermelon and split for his truck. A lot of the food was left behind. What we left behind, too, was a lot of confused people. Most of them didn't know where we came from and very few knew where we were going. Fire-fighting by busted campers was done on a low profile basis. We rarely got any press or credit for our work.

We ended up in the hills close by Ventura County. All kinds of crews were there. No goofing off by anyone. We wondered out loud what the big deal was. Why would anyone get excited about a fire in a place where there were only hills, no homes and only scrub brush.

At six o'clock p.m. that Friday evening, Horvath conferred with the F.O.'s from Campo Tres. They called over Dedrick, Garcia and Little. These guys were graduating and if they had been in camp, they would have been having supper and listening to goodbye speeches.

Horvath asked them if they smoked. They all said a cautious yes. "Okay, amigos, we are going to take time off to eat, then we have to hit the fire lines again until we're relieved. I'm going to make a ruling in your cases. By the time we finish eating, your time in camp should be over. We will say goodbye to you, and we have voted to let you have your first legal smoke in several months. You suckers have earned it." It may not seem like a big deal now, but it was a big deal at the time.

What a charge everyone got out of that. Horvath sent the three of them to sit in the portable head to smoke, so as not to contaminate our morals. I guess he wasn't sure of his legal ground. If nobody said anything, then nothing happened. The old man was okay, I knew it. Some of the other guys were starting to know it also.

One odd thing about this p.m.'s graduation exercise; all three of the guys who were graduating had ended up on the ding crew for one reason or another. On top of that, they had made more time than necessary through personal stupidity or an inability to meet the demands of the camp program. They were lucky to have escaped losing their graduation date. I suppose it was because they were immature, more than mean, except in Dedrick's case. He could be mean when pushed to it or when he didn't understand something enough to deal with it.

∘   ∘   ∘

We were finally relieved. The ride home on the bouncing back of the truck was a drag. I was able to sleep some, but between the bouncing and my catching a couple of guys trying to light up, it wasn't a smooth ride back. I had to shit on the guys who tried smoking. I let them know. "I'll turn your asses in. I'm not going to lose being mayor or lose my date for no stupid asses." This position on my part was dangerous for me, 'cause I was dealing with dings and new people who didn't know or believe in the camp culture yet. If they chose to back up the smoker's play, my ass was grass.

The smokers backed down from me, but not before they studied me for a few minutes. I realized even as I spoke that they couldn't give a damn about my position. If they cared, they wouldn't be on the ding crew. "You hassle me here, and when we get to camp, you'll have my boys to worry about. I promise you you'll get your asses kicked in."

Peer pressure won out. They backed off. The rest of the crew relaxed. I stayed hot. I wondered whether or not I should follow up with each of these smokers on a one-to-one basis. I couldn't decide whether to let it slide or challenge them. Horvath and what the staff stood for was on one side of my conscience. On the other side was the fact that, as I saw it, if I didn't challenge them individually, my last week in camp might be a disaster. These two jerks could put a jacket on me as a cheese-eating sissy. Loss of face with my bunkies could follow. "What should I do?" Once again I was between a rock and a hard place.

We finally got to camp. About two o'clock in the morning, Horvath came around and dropped the steps. I hurried down and gave some orders. "Step down, line up, get your distance, pick your heads up and listen. All right Mr. Horvath, they're yours."

Horvath looked at me, then back at the group. "You suckers did a good job. We're sorry you're in so late, but that's the breaks. Garcia, Dedrick and Little, stay behind. The rest of you, go on in. Fill your canteens, use the head and crap out."

We went into the dorm, did as directed and then crashed. Before I fell asleep, I decided what I would do. This had to be taken care of either Saturday or Sunday.

I decided to sleep through breakfast. By the time I got up, made it to the showers and back again to my sack, some of the guys had come to me and asked how I was going to handle the dings who had given me the hard time. Once again Johnson was cool, telling me he'd go with whatever I decided. Baldwin wanted to help me to kick ass and he would be there with me. Some of the Chicanos came by for some small talk. They were waiting to hear what kind of court I was going to conduct. They couldn't come out and ask, but the question was in their eyes and in what they were not asking. What a barrio culture, where you can't really come out and compromise a person by asking. They knew what space between people was.

Up to this point, only Horvath had caught a glimpse that all was not groovy. He had seen it last night. By now he probably had forgotten. None of the other staff smelled anything. As for the two smokers, they were lucky they weren't from the Cougars, or else they would have been made Christians very early.

As it was, the Bears had one of the guys and the Trojans had another. The boy leaders came by to find out how things would be handled. I was assured that there would be no finking. I wondered how the smokers felt by now. They were probably feeling some pressure. I sure was feeling some myself. This was something I couldn't shine on.

How things can escalate from insignificant incidents to something that becomes important to many is really strange and still hard to fathom. Originally, I had figured this would be quiet business between two fools and me. I had to psych myself up to the challenge and then carry out the threat to kick ass if the two didn't back down. Or, I had the right, I supposed, to turn my back, take responsibility and report the action.

After lunch, I asked Johnson to check out the shower room

and then behind the shower. He said, "I get you, brother."
He checked it out, came back and said that the dorm boy said
things would be cool. He would handle anybody coming in. I
called the boy leader from the Bears over.

"Look here, man, go down and tell the ding to slip over
behind the shower building. I'll be there by the time he gets
there."

"Okay, man, but what if he won't come out?"

"Well, then, knock him on his ass in front of the rest of
the guys. I told him if he didn't lighten up, the *batos* would
handle it. I'm sure he'd rather face me than you.

I got up off my sack and kind of meandered out of the dorm
to the shower room and out the back door. Behind the shower
building was the traditional place to settle disputes in an honorable form. Staff had been known not to know what the haps
were by staying away, not looking and not knowing until in-
house politics were settled. Whether staff was hip to what was
happening or not, I didn't know. By now, I had made up my
mind to follow through with a one-on-one confrontation. I
had pumped myself up and I was getting high for a beef.

The ding showed up.

"You want to see me?"

"Yeah, you were bad last night. I figure I don't need the
camp to handle your ass, but I didn't want to hit you up in
public, 'cause you'd probably go around saying that I only took
you 'cause you were scared of getting rat packed. Jump bad
with me now, punk."

I grated the words, had my hands up and was pushing on
him. I chested him as much as I could. He started to talk
and I cut him off. "I ain't here to talk, shithead. You throw a
punch or tell me you're going to knock off your shit on crew
and around camp."

He backed off. "Aw, man, I was tired last night and should
have known better. Things will be cool from now on." He
said a few more things that I really didn't hear.

I told him, "Split, I'll watch you and your partner from now
on."

He split. "Wow, one down and one more to go."

I called the dorm boy from the showers. "Hey, cool, get the
Trojan boy leader out here."

"Okay, mayor, I'll be right back with him."

The Trojan B.L. came into the shower room.

"Look here, man, I want your man out here. I don't know where he stands with you. I know you guys kind of get along, but I got to cover my action. You want to send him out?"

"Yeah, boss, I'll get him for you, but can I be here with you? You know, he's kind of slow and needs someone to talk for him sometimes," he said.

"Hey man, has anyone pushed him around or hit him in his mouth?"

"No, man, they haven't," he replied.

"Well, then he's overdue. Go get him and, no, I want to see him alone," I said.

The next ding showed up. Dingy as this fool was, he still surprised me.

"Hi mayor, what's going on? B.L. said you wanted to see me."

"Yeah, stupid," I spit out. "I want to get straight with you over last night. I'm not going to talk. I'm going to kick your ass for you, so you don't try messing with me in public anymore."

"What the hell you talking about?" he shot back.

I hit him while he was still talking, then I kicked him in the stomach. I backed off and waited to see what he would do. I expected that as soon as he got his breath, he would leave or charge me. He charged me. I stepped to one side and, as he went by, I hit him in the small of the back. This knocked him down. He lost his wind and anymore ideas of getting at me. With this punk, I didn't know where I would stand the next week.

I hollered for the dorm boy and told him, "Get the B.L." He came and I told him, "Walk back into the dorm with this ding. If you want him to finish his camp time, you keep him cool and teach him some manners. I didn't give him too much. If he learned something, he'll be okay. If not, I feel for him."

The B.L. looked like he wanted to do me a number, but said nothing to me. To the ding he said, "Come on, stupid, let's get back to the dorm."

They both went out. I sat down on an upturned barrel. Suddenly I felt drained. I sure didn't enjoy that ... or did I? In a way I did. I had tested myself and made it through. I could hold my head up among my peers. I hoped there was no avenging angel close by. There wasn't.

I made it over to the Cougar's end of the dorm and on to my bed. I laid there looking up at the ceiling, my hands clasped behind my head. "Damn, I been lying on this bed looking up at the ceiling for months, trying to work things out or checking myself out. I'm going to miss this spot," I thought.

Johnson came by, looked down and said, "You a bad mother, little man," and walked off. I didn't feel like a bad anything. I do know I felt at ease. My anxiety was over.

o   o   o

Later that day we made it to town hall. I had to get up and give a speech on how the camp was doing. I brought out some shortcomings on the part of the staff. This was cheered. I talked about camp positions and who held them and how I appreciated their cooperation.

From there I spotlighted some examples of cheese eating and how it did not help the camp culture. I asked for comments from the floor. I got plenty, some directed at me, some at the staff, and some at the cook and his work force. That was what town hall was all about. Some of the staff made some observations and then we adjourned.

o   o   o

The day ended, the night came. The night ended, the day came. We went through our Sunday without the visitors routine. For the Protestants, there were services in camp. They had some good services. You found Catholics going to Protestant services because the Protestants had no kneeling, they sang a lot, their sermons were short and in English and, best of all, they brought along a few girls. The girls seemed devoted to their religion and nobody tried to mess with them, but they were looking good. Even if the conversation was about Jesus Christ, it was still a conversation with a girl. Anyway, what was wrong with talking to nice girls about clean subjects? As the mayor, I was allowed the leeway of playing host. I enjoyed this.

There was another attraction, in terms of being Catholic. If you signed up in advance, you were allowed to travel out of camp to services in the little village of Malibu. It had been established that you didn't use religion as an excuse to leave. Whether a guy was on the shit list or not, he had the right to religious instruction.

On this trip to church, I was more careful than even the P.O.'s with the guys. I was very much aware that this was my last Sunday in camp. I wanted to cram everything into it, experience-wise. A sadness was settling in. A kind of sweet sadness, because while I was losing something I had become very fond of, I also was looking with a great deal of anticipation toward an unencumbered life on the outs very soon.

I wandered over to the playing field. I watched the guys play softball. After a while, I joined in. They were playing "work up." It was fun. Time went by, supper came and went. Since the daylight stayed around until eight o'clock, we were allowed to stay out of doors. This was nice. We went back to singing the barrio songs accompanied by the guitars.

Nine o'clock and we were in bed or getting ready for bed and lights out. The night man played a few records, then turned the radio on to a station that played a variety of music. The music was woven into my thoughts and then dreams.

○   ○   ○

It was Monday and my last full week in camp. "Lord help me through this last hurdle, this last ordeal. I swear I'll be good. I swear if I'm not, I'll make it up to you. Oh, what a big hypocrite. The only time I remember Him is when I'm hurting," I thought to myself.

Crew was uneventful. Everything that had to be taken care of had been. I had made the right decision. The crew did not goof off. Miles, who rode out with us, commented to Wells that he had never seen a more cooperative group, especially for a Monday. Wells agreed and hoped it would continue all week. For my part, I knew it was an easy skate. Every crew member was hip to what had to be.

Late that afternoon, five campers split from camp. None of the guys were vets, but all of them were Chicanos. What a drag. Later on, Horvath gave me the details. He laughed as he told me how the O.D., Cristos, had chased them until he stood on top of a hill and watched them run down a ravine.

He had hollered down to them, "Come back, don't be fools, don't bring down the *raza*." (Imagine Cristos laying a "raza" trip on them.) Anyway, one of the dudes who split, turned around, gave him the jug sign and kept on running.

Cristos had almost flipped, according to Horvath. He recovered and went off to call the sheriff. This had bothered the staff, because they wanted to try to catch the guys first. If they had, they would have kept everything in-house. With the sheriff called in, there had to be special reports.

The runaway shouldn't have given Cristos the jug sign. Cristos wasn't too tolerant of those who showed disrespect for his position.

As I heard it later, the sheriff caught those dudes, then called the camp. Cristos asked them to bring the runaways in. They did. They brought the staff down for their lax way of handling inmates and left, telling the staff they would be available, if needed.

Cristos stood those five suckers at attention. He read them off and finally called down to Juvie. He let them know that he was returning five campers. This was a bring-down for the camp. You never did things like this. It was a bigger bring-down for the *raza*. The *raza* never quit a camp like this. What a drag.

I heard later that two of them came back to Campo Tres. I wonder if Cristos had a fit. I bet he did.

∘ ∘ ∘

The week ended and here I was on my way down to the staff office with Mr. Horvath. It was hard to believe. My graduation jacket with its certificate and all the autographs were tucked under my arm. I took a lot of deep breaths of some real fine country night air. I was trying to cram in some remembrances so that later on when nostalgia set in, all of this would be clear to me. "Goodbye forever, Campo Tres, I'll miss you," I said to myself.

Chapter XVIII

There was not too much to the trip from camp to downtown Los Angeles. From L.A. to the pad was a different story. The car wanted to go across the river to the city on the other side. It would have too, if I hadn't been reminded that we were living on the south side. My pop gently told me, "We don't live on the east side anymore. We moved to the south side. As a matter of fact, I saved for a down payment and bought two houses on a lot." So, instead of going over the bridge to the city across the river, I turned right on San Pedro Street and headed south.

By now it was after nine at night. It wasn't really late, but inside my system was saying that it was. Back in camp the guys were in bed or getting ready for it. They were asking the night man to play some good sounds. They'd be finishing up in the head. Some of them were rolling a cigarette along the floor to a friend they owed a favor to. The guys that slept at the end of the dorm probably had a cigarette going. They would take a toke and fan the air at the same time, so it wasn't noticeable. I remembered the smoke hanging heavy and how easy it was to spot if the night man was observant. I tried to shake loose these thoughts, mostly because we had been chattering along. "They don't know what I'm thinking. They're worried 'cause they feel I might not want to communicate, maybe shut them out."

San Pedro Street was humming with people. I noticed as I turned onto it that the Japanese people were gone from Little Tokyo. They were put in "relocation centers." This was done at first because the Paddys felt that they were all loyal to the Rising Sun and would be spies for Japan. Later, they explained that it was done for their protection.

After all, we, the citizens, hated them because they were

sneaky and had killed a lot of Americans. The stories in the paper about Japs were there all the time, helping us to hate. The movies were generally war stories. If they weren't about Europe and the Germans, then they were about the Sons of Nippon versus "Our Boys in Uniform" in the South Pacific. I can still remember a series of pictures about the South Pacific, such as "Bataan," "Behind the Rising Sun," "Thirty Seconds Over Tokyo," and others. Then too, the Bowery Boys and other American heroes were battling would-be saboteurs in the good old U.S.A.

In place of the Japanese, there were mostly black people now living in the hotels and apartments. They seemed to have taken over the small restaurants and "juice" joints as well. The music coming out into the night sounded groovy.

Down San Pedro, between Eighth and Olympic, the people who worked the food docks were standing around waiting to go to work. In those days there was work for everybody, so if a wino wanted to work to make money for grape juice, nobody would ask if he had a high school diploma before he hired on as a swamper.

There were Chinese restaurants lining the streets. In between, there were Mexican restaurants. Talk about weird musical sounds. How about a mariachi that sounded Chinese?

A few blocks down and we were going through an area that was highly populated and at the same time was commercial in nature. There were furniture factories, gas stations, grocery stores, bars and small hotels. We passed Jefferson Avenue. Some of the guys from Twenty-Second hung around there. Their graffiti indicated this. I knew a couple of guys from there. They were nice guys. There weren't too many of them. They were busy trying to make a name for themselves. They were pinched in by the guys from Santa Barbara Avenue, the guys from Thirty-eighth and the guys from Clanton. In this area the guys went to Jefferson High School, if they got that far, and to Lafayette Jr. High School. Sometimes they got it on in school, but most of the time the action took place on the streets and at house parties. They were no different than the barrios in East Los Angeles.

We crossed Santa Barbara Avenue. The barrio took its name from the street. It was shortened to S.B.A. These guys had become our enemies for some reason. It might have been a beef at the Sons of Herman Ballroom. They kind of controlled the action there and they might have had a run-in with some of our *batos*. Since I had gone to John Adams Jr. High School, I knew some of these guys, but that hadn't meant anything to them once our beef started. I was from T-Flats and that's all that mattered. They had made this clear to me one day at Metro.

A few blocks and we were on the west side of Thirty-eighth Street territory. This barrio was now famous because of the Sleepy Lagoon murder case. I watched this case closely, reading the paper and talking to some of the people from that neighborhood. I had three cousins who claimed Thirty-eighth Street as their barrio. One of them got busted, along with twenty others for the murder of some dude at a kind of night picnic party. When it first happened, the newspaper accounts weren't clear. Those who got busted weren't allowed to talk to anyone. They weren't allowed out on bail. By the time the dust was settled, some sixteen guys were convicted of a murder which was never proven, and they were sent off to San Quentin. Some three or four girls were sent off to Youth Authority Facilities for Girls. These girls truly were not involved. I guess our justice system felt compelled to teach them a lesson for hanging around with the wrong crowd.

What really hung on our heads was the bald-faced admission on the part of a judge that he didn't like Mexicans. During the trial those guys, besides not being allowed bail, were not allowed to shave or wash. They were also not allowed a change of clothes. The prejudiced newspapers had a ball with that. They were allowed to take all the pictures they wanted of these poor suckers. These pictures were fed to a public willing to believe any and all slanderous remarks.

I wonder how many hundreds of young Chicanos and Chicanas grew chips on their shoulders because of what happened during those times. There were severe cases of racial prejudice in reverse and extreme cases of paranoia, because we could do nothing but strike out blindly. And the penalty was generally a broken spirit and retreat to a barrio, never to come out again. Then, as those persons married and had children, they passed their prejudice and sense of futility along to their children.

I turned the car down Compton Avenue, then to our street. We were living on Fifty-ninth Place. There were two houses on the lot. There were garages for two cars, a front lawn, hedges and a large tree in front.

I parked the car in the driveway. We got out and, after my father unlocked the door, we went in. They took me around the house. The main attraction was my bedroom. I'd be sharing it with my brother, but that wouldn't be too bad. My sister had her own room and then my folks had theirs. They were quite proud of their new possession. The house was nice inside and out.

Around eleven o'clock that evening I started to get antsy. I wanted to make it to the corner, but felt guilty. I'd been away over seven months and finally I was with the only people who really cared about me—and here I was getting itchy. I tried to relax and couldn't. We had a phone now, so I asked to use it and pulled out some phone numbers. Johnny wasn't home. I passed Penny's number, 'cause I wanted to save that for during the week. After a while, I just sat talking with the folks.

We talked about work. I would have to go out soon and look for a job. My pop felt I could probably get a job washing dishes or as a busboy. It sounded like a drag. He tried to tell me that I could probably move up real fast if the boss liked me. I didn't tell him no. What I said was that I had to think about different types of work and then I had to clear it with my probation officer. He had to approve of the job I took. I also had to check into school.

"Look son," he said, "school is not for Mexicans. It's a waste of time. What you need to do is get a job in a factory. Once there, you should work to become the foreman's right hand man. Be valuable to him and he'll take care of you. If you have to be up, use your time making money. Going to school is not going to put any money in your pocket or in the bank."

I thought about what he said. I wished I could say he was wrong and show him as an example some Mexican who had made it because of education. I couldn't come up with anyone.

Well, the hell with it. If I got a chance I would sneak in some school time. I would also get a job. If I got bored, I'd join the service. This would be one way of leaving the pad legitimately.

Momma had sat listening to the conversation that went on between my father and me. She was glad we were talking, but was monitoring us, just in case one or the other of us got too heavy with our personal views. I know this was what she was into. I wondered if my father had picked this up too. He didn't indicate anything. She chimed in by saying she was glad to have me home. She hoped that I had learned my lesson and wouldn't end up in jail again.

I told them, "I liked the camp life, but not Juvie or Hollenbeck. To my way of thinking, I didn't do too much wrong. If I had to do it over again, I would. I still don't feel like a criminal. A criminal to me is a thief or murderer for gain, or a doper. I'm not anything like that and I don't intend to be anything like that."

It kind of squelched her, but since I said it in a quiet manner, I don't think I hurt her. I was serious, though. I might continue hanging out with the *batos locos* from my barrio. I might go for the "crazy life," but it didn't mean I would be a total waste.

We talked about Pablo, my brother. He had me going. I didn't know what our first meeting was going to be like. It was no secret by now that he had my mother and father climbing the walls because of his actions. This guy had been handled with more consideration than my sister or me. He had me pissed off. My feelings were hurt because I had expected he would be with the folks when they went to pick me up. I knew if he had been in my place, I would have been there. From what I had heard lately about Pablo's dealings in the neighborhood, he wasn't doing good things. Momma talked about his getting suspended from school. It finally came out that he was blowing a joint during football practice. Needless to say, he was no longer on the football team. Jefferson High School wanted no one like that playing for them. For good measure, they kicked him out of school for two weeks. He was lucky they didn't blow the whistle on him. The cops at Georgia Street Juvenile would have enjoyed his company.

I guess what really bugged me was that I truly liked him. On top of that, I always had the feeling that he wanted to live up to my reputation. In a way he wanted to keep my name up there among the bad. At this point, even though he was just getting to be sixteen years old, he was looking for his own identity. Like me, he hadn't found it in school or with the straight folks in the neighborhood. He had found it in the *batos locos*. The only difference was that he didn't know when to stop. He wasn't too cool about choosing partners. He also didn't know when to quit and split for home. What the hell was I talking about. Here I was moralizing about him. I should look in the mirror.

○   ○   ○

When I woke up the next morning, I noticed that Pablo was lying in his bed. His dark glasses were on over his eyes. He was fast asleep. Funny, I hadn't heard him come in and he didn't bother to wake me up. He was probably stoned and in no mood to hear a lecture. I figured I'd wake him up after I cleaned up. It was still early, only eight o'clock—although it was late by the camp clock, especially for a Monday. I headed for the bathroom, took a bath—something which I'd been looking forward to for a long time. Showers are great, but every now and then you want to lie around soaking. I got out reluctantly and dried up. I put on shorts and then looked in the mirror as I put tooth powder in my left hand, wet my brush with my right hand, then scraped the powder up and did a job on my teeth. The powder almost always made me gag. But clean teeth and fresh breath were important to me. It gave me confidence. I could smile freely.

I looked at my face, ran my hand lightly over it, checking out the pimples. There weren't that many. There was a stubble of beard on my jaw and just a bit on my cheeks by my sideburns. I shaved this off, but left some on above my upper lip. I wanted to get a mustache as soon as possible. I hoped I'd gotten more in the past seven months. I had heard that it would grow thicker if you shaved daily. I also had heard that if you rubbed garlic on that spot, the hair would get thick. I never tried this, but I had thought of doing it a time or two. I figured it was nothing but a put-on by some of the older guys. I didn't want to get caught behind their bull.

Next I checked out my hair. It was close-cropped, not quite a butch haircut and not quite a two line cut. I reached for the Dixie Pomade jar. It was time to start retraining my hair back to the "ducktail" style. I took it easy and didn't put too much on. I'd gotten out of the habit and the stuff felt greasy. Combing it back on the sides got me nothing. It was still too short. "Oh well, I'll be back in style in a week or two."

I hollered out, "Hey, Mom, I'm up, can I have a pair of khakis to wear?" She had figured I might want to wear khakis. She brought them in all nice and pressed, including a crease down the front that really stuck out. They were well starched. My mom was getting pretty good at it, probably because Pablo stayed on her to do the job right. She asked about a shirt and handed me a grey Arrow. It fit snug but looked good on me. It showed that I had filled out. I could show off my new physique without being obvious.

I went back to the bedroom, picked up a pillow and smacked Pablo in the face with it. He came around slowly. He stared at me through his tea-timers for a while. Finally he focused in on me and smiled.

"What's to it, brother? Good to see you at home. What you got planned for today? I got some ideas for us, especially if you want to get into the swing of things right away." He said all of this in a kind of train of words.

I stood looking over him. "I'm going to eat," I said. "Then I got some things I got to take care of."

About that time, my mom called that the breakfast was on the table. I hadn't asked for anything special, whatever she whipped up would be good. Camp food was great, but this was Momma cooking.

"Let me eat first, then we can talk. In the meantime, if you want to, you can get ready, too, and you can go with me." I added that I would need some help cleaning the car, 'cause I didn't want to cruise around in a dirty car. He got the message, started to deny fault, but thought better of it.

The breakfast consisted of eggs, beans, chopped meat and potatoes. She had made tortillas to go with it. I drank milk. We didn't do much talking while I ate. She had brought us up to eat without talking, but this wasn't the reason I didn't talk now. I wanted to savor the food, and conversation would have interfered with my concentration.

"How about a little chile, Momma?" I asked.

She went to the refrigerator and brought some out, along with a spoon. That was good too, not too hot, but just enough bite on the tongue. When I finished, she asked if I wanted any dessert. I told her no, that the food had filled me up. It was just what I wanted and I thanked her. She seemed pleased to hear the praise. I wondered idly if anyone was saying nice things to her lately. I'd have to watch and listen to see how she was being treated.

Being busted gave you a deep appreciation for your mother and what she means to you, what she gives of herself to her offspring and to her spouse. No wonder there are so many songs and poems written about these kind ladies who are often much maligned and abused by selfish family members who have not had to do without them. I promised myself that I was going to be good to her, watch out for her interests and not let anyone take advantage of her.

I went out to the garage for my car. I got in, backed it out, ran the motor until it was warm, then turned it off. I got out, walked around looking at the paint job, the dings in the body, looked at the wheel with the missing hub cap, and finally at the canvas roof of my convertible. I had feared the worst, but it wasn't too bad. I figured that I'd get a report from Pablo on my car. It would be all excuses, for sure. While I waited for him, I cleaned out the inside of the car with a whisk broom, then dusted the dashboard and washed the windows. I lowered and raised the convertible top to see if it was operating all right. I concluded that it needed some oiling in the joints. I left the top down, got a bucket, filled it with water and dipped a chamois in it.

I was finishing the job when Pablo walked out ready to help me. I'd gotten caught up in what I was doing and he knew it. This was like the old days. He was never available when there was dirty work to be done. I ran all this down to him, while he stood there looking hurt that I would even think anything like this about him. I warmed to the subject at hand.

"Why the hell did you let the car get this run down? To begin with, I never gave you permission to drive the damn car. You pushed on my mother to let you use it, then you didn't have the decency to at least take care of it. As far as I'm concerned, I'll give you a ride if you want one, but you're not going to drive this car anymore."

He started to protest his innocence.

I said, "Cut your shit. I'm not having any."

He stared at me for a while. He probably wanted to challenge what I said. I stared back at him so that he would know I wasn't jiving him.

I went in the house, changed T-shirts and put on my ironed Arrow shirt. I told my mother I would be home later, at the latest by supper time.

"You going, Pablo?" I asked.

He nodded and got in the car.

I told him, "We'll go to the neighborhood first, and drop you off, then I'll go take care of my business."

He agreed to that. He didn't particularly want to go to the probation office and the school office. Personally, I had expected to take care of business first and then head for the corner, but I had to admit that I wanted to see what was happening as soon as possible. I was really itching to get there.

Chapter XIX

I wanted to walk around on Fourth Street. I figured that I'd even bounce for some booze if the guys were broke. This reminded me that I hadn't had a beer in months. My mouth kind of puckered at the thought of a Lucky sliding down my throat. I pressed down on the gas pedal.

We got to Olympic and Soto. On the left, Sears and Roebuck had grown bigger. They were expanding as they got more customers. Probably by the time they got through, everyone on the Eastside would be into them for a piece of change. Well, they had merchandise at reasonable prices. I was glad a good big store had decided to settle here. As we neared Whittier and Soto, I tried to judge the signal to make it on the go sign, if not, not to get boxed in between a car in front and back. The *batos* around here were still our enemies and plenty of them knew both of us. If they were around, they would jump us. I had put most of that away while I was busted, but I was out now and my jungle instincts were back with me.

"Keep your eyes open for any of them nuts from Hoyo Soto. I don't want to get caught by them now. I can just see us get into a beef on my first day out. The fuzz would love it."

"Don't worry about it, brother, I have a few *camaradas* in this barrio. We get along real well."

"Well, maybe you do, but I don't have friends here. If it's all the same to you, I don't want to meet anyone just now."

I made a right turn on Whittier Boulevard. This took us right through the heart of Hoyo Soto.

"I thought you weren't looking for problems? What you doing driving down this road?"

Some guys were standing on the corner of Orme, looking bad in their drapes and dark shirts. They gave us the finger and hollered at us to come back. I shined them on. Pablo gave them the jug sign and laughed at them. We continued down Whittier past the YMCA and then came to Euclid and turned left. On the left side of the street there was a dime store. When I was small I had worked there on Saturday mornings, sweeping and dusting. They paid me twenty-five cents. When I left there, I would walk on down the street with my shoeshine box looking for customers.

Across the street was the Euclid Avenue Elementary School. I had graduated from Euclid, voted the most likely to succeed, with a string of perfect report cards. My reward for perfect report cards came from my cousin Emilia. We would dress up, then she would take me to the dime store and let me pick any present I wanted. Afterward, she would take me downtown to see a movie of my choice.

I parked the car on Fourth and Fresno. Pablo went off down Fourth Street after saying, "See you later, alligator." I hung around. In about a half hour or so the guys began showing up. They each shook hands with me in a kind of formal manner. We seemed a little stiff with each other. It was not too macho to show emotion. These guys had been with me the night of the Big Zoot Suit vs. Servicemen fight in T.F. that had led to my getting busted. They had followed my case. For sure, they wondered whether or not I would cop out on them. The time had passed. They weren't bothered and I was out. I was glad the cops hadn't pressed me that hard to find out who was with me. Not that I would have ratted, but it could have been uncomfortable. We had developed a reputation with the police, though. If we were caught, we would take the consequences. They didn't have to work hard to get an admission, but we never took anyone with us, if we could help it. The cops seemed to appreciate this.

A lot of times they had dragged a bunch of guys into a station for some violation of the law. The cops would lay out the facts, then ask if anyone wanted to "take the rap." If someone came forward and admitted guilt, the rest would be cut loose. They generally kept their word. They really didn't care if the guilty party came forward. They just wanted a body to convict. The courts didn't look that carefully at the evidence and the defense attorneys weren't about to buck the system. They wouldn't get any business breaks if they got a reputation of trying to make the cops and district attorneys look bad.

We talked and walked. We traded stories. I told them about Topo and the beef he had and how he ended up being sent to Preston. They told me about all the guys who had gone into the service. We laid on the lawn of the Russian's house across the street from the Malt Shop. They had me repeat the story of my camp time. I recounted a few adventures. All of the guys, except Art, had been to Juvie, so we compared notes.

The tomatoes started coming by. The clothes styles hadn't changed much for the girls. As they came by I was surprised at how much some of them had ripened while I was away. But even though I said cool things to their behinds as they wiggled by, I still felt self-conscious. They were going to school, so that meant that they were virgins and I was too old for them.

Alicia came by with some of her friends. She was the most popular among the guys. Other girls always came around with her, so they could make out. We talked for a while. I asked her for her brother. She said he was through with basic training and getting ready to ship out overseas. He was in some place in New Jersey. He wasn't too lonely, 'cause David from Geraghty was with him. I told her I knew about David, 'cause we were writing. I asked if she had seen Martha; her baby was due and I had to see her. She hadn't seen her, but was willing to go with me when I got ready.

I asked Alicia about school. "Was it nice? Are you going to graduate? What are you studying?"

She said, "I'm a senior now and it's fun. We're not learning too much, because they aren't teaching too much. Maybe it's the war. The teachers don't have their mind on their work. The students try, but for the most part, we don't really give a damn. I'm going to graduate, 'cause there is nothing else happening. I'll probably get a job in some factory. In a way, it isn't a bring down, 'cause everybody's getting jobs like that. I'll have plenty of company and if I get ambitious, I might really learn to type and move into the front office. Clerks don't make as much as factory workers, but they get to dress nice and it makes the family feel important."

A couple of girls came over and stood around listening to us talk. I offered them a coke or a malt and got introduced to them in the process. One of the girls was named Rachel. She was nice-looking and kind of forward.

"Hey, *ese*, how come you got short hair and how come I haven't seen you around?"

She wanted to know if I was a new boy trying to get into the barrio. This bothered the shit out of me. Here I was a bonafide vet, having been through a bust, in countless gang fights, knew all the main places, dressed up to date and had chicks anytime I wanted them, and this bitty broad was ranking me. I stared at her and decided to shine her on.

I turned to Alicia, "Hey, get this student off my back."

Alicia took Rachel and her malt off to put nickels in the juke box. She probably would bring her up to date. With this done, my bruised ego would be soothed.

This left me looking at Penny. I looked her over. She hadn't changed that much, maybe filled out a bit more. For my part, I wanted to drink her in a bit more before I said anything. My heart was thumping. I thought I had gotten her out of my system. At this point, it was obvious I hadn't. She looked Chicana or Italian. She was nice-looking in a quiet way. She hadn't said anything to me yet.

One thing for sure, she was not my type of girl, especially not now. Right now, I was a guy on the make. I kept checking her out as we small-talked. I sneaked looks, really. She wasn't small, but she wasn't big either.

She told me, "I really like school now. I'm interested in being a part of the student council. I'm a senior, too. I'll graduate with Alicia this February. I expect to go to college."

She was getting me interested in what she was talking about. At first, I had answered her with shuck and jive, but now I started paying attention. I dredged up what I remembered of high school, then continuation school and what I had learned in camp from Fisher. I found myself trying to impress her.

I ended up repeating to her what she already knew: that I had quit school in the tenth grade after I had turned sixteen, and that before that I had been a good student, even making A's in school in subjects like history, math and the like. I said, "When I was in Junior High School, I palled around with this square Paddy dude who always talked about college. I liked listening to him. I made up my mind that the two of us would go together. I didn't know college from something out of space. But when I talked to that dude, it seemed like it could be for me too. I used to tell Neil—that was the kid's name—that if he could go there, so could I. To him it was a fact of life, to me it was fantasy."

We danced a couple of slow dances. We were self-conscious. I found myself putting her back on a pedestal, kind of out of reach. She was clean, but wonder of wonders, she seemed genuinely interested in what I had to say. It was as if we were meeting for the first time, instead of having gone somewhat steady before I had gotten busted.

I didn't bring up the fact that we had shined each other on for nearly a year and neither did she. I didn't want to explain myself and, I guess, she didn't want to hear any bull. That was good.

Later, as Alicia, Rachel and Penny were getting ready to leave, I asked Penny, "Can I walk you home?"

She said no, "It was nice talking to you and all that, but there's no use taking it past that."

I persisted, "How come it's all right to talk to you here, but it ain't all right to walk you home?"

She answered, "We had a good thing going before, but that's the past. Let's just stay friends. You know Angel, my brother, he told me to stay away from you guys. I do what he says. You're all nice guys. He hangs around with you, but I can't. He told my parents to watch over me and not let me date any of the guys. It was for my own good."

She didn't throw my getting busted in my face, but I got the picture.

I held her hand, looked at her face, and ended up by telling her that her brother was right. "We're a bunch of losers going nowhere. I'm glad I got to see you again. I'm sorry I bothered you. Goodbye." I turned from the three girls and walked away towards where some of the *batos* were standing by the juke box.

Alicia called out, "Hey, Mikie, there's a party at my pad this weekend. You make it over."

I thanked her for the invite and told her I would be there.

Rachel surprised me by saying, "I'm glad I met you and I'll mess around with you anytime, 'cause you're from a good barrio."

I figured it was more of a dig at Penny, who she probably considered a big square. Penny didn't say anything. She didn't even say goodbye.

Well, if I hadn't thought of lushing since I got home the day before, at least not seriously, I suddenly did then.

I wouldn't make it to the P.O.'s office or even to the School Board that day. So I thought that I would see what was happening, and if nothing was happening, I would make it happen.

"Hey Art, let's pick up some Dago Red and some beer and have a party or something. How about the rest of you guys? You want to get loaded?"

"Why not," said Johnny, "I got some bread and the rest of these guys can chip in too."

"What about chicks?" he asked.

"I don't know about chicks for tonight, man. Why not just get lushed up and live up the good old days? Maybe after, we can throw a cruise around and see what develops."

"All right," and like Pancho tells the Cisco Kid, Art said "Let's went brother."

Art, Johnny and Beaver walked out with me towards the car. It was time to get high. The guys jumped in the car. We drove over to Lincoln Heights. Beaver, who liked wine, knew all the private homes where we could get a gallon of wine. We stopped at a house near Avenue 20. We collected a dollar and a half among us and gave it to Beaver, who walked down the street.

While we waited, we talked. Johnny wanted to know, "You blow pot?" I asked him what that was. "What a dummy, that's another name for weed, man."

"No, I'm still on the same kick. I still don't believe in it."

"Well, I'm sorry for you, man," he said, " 'cause all of us blow pot now and if you want to be with us, you're going to learn to use it."

I told him, "Look, man, if it comes to picking between pot and being a part of the barrio, I might have to split, 'cause I ain't going to let anything I can't control get inside my body. If you don't want to be with me, that's okay with me. By the way, since when do you decide policy for the barrio?"

He shut up.

Three guys passed by. They were draped out and walked like they were in their own neighborhood. They looked us over. We didn't recognize them and they didn't seem to know us either. We figured they were from Clover, but from a younger clique. They kept on walking. They seemed to be making up their minds what to do. I got fidgety. I suddenly started hoping that Beaver would get here in a big hurry.

The three started back towards us. It looked like they had made up their minds what to do. As they got closer, I noticed they were younger than us, maybe between fourteen and sixteen.

"Where you from?" the older looking *bato* asked.

Art and Johnny gave them a chicken-shit smile. I looked away, playing the bored part, but keeping my ears open to what was said.

"Look here, *carnales*," Art said, "we're waiting for our partner to get here with some Dago Red. When he gets here, we'll split."

Johnny cut in, "You want to know where we're from, but you ain't told us where you're from. You let us know what barrio you claim and maybe we'll tell you where we're from."

I could see that Art and Johnny were not going to back down from these kids. The kids could be dangerous if they were carrying knives, because they would use them if they got scared. If they weren't carrying anything and wanted to fight, they were about to get their asses kicked. The three kids were standing there uncertain as to what to do.

In the meantime, Beaver showed up with our wine. He acted as if he didn't see our opposition. I asked him for one bottle, took off the cork and took a good swig. I offered it to the talking one of the three.

"Take a snort on us and, by the way, we're from T-Flats and we're partners with the older *batos* from Clover."

They took the bottle and each one took a swig and passed the bottle back to Art. Art put the cork in the bottle without drinking. He smiled at the three and said, "I want you fools to see this gun. The next time I see you or you see me, I'm going to use it on you. You better pick up on what's happening and not mess with people unless you know them or they're your age. If not, you're not going to get any older. Now get the hell away from us."

He looked at me and I started the car and drove slowly off. About a block away, I started to crack up. Art had been cool. Those little boys didn't know whether to shit or go blind. I was sure they had learned a lesson. They were probably the little brother's of some of the guys we knew, and they would be telling them about us and asking for support. We'd see what would happen. Probably nothing. We turned down Fourth towards the corner. As we drove, we drank out of the jug.

"Where we going when we get to the corner?" I asked.

Art said, "Let's go down the gulley and see what's there. If we don't find anyone, we'll go to the end of the block and just sit around and drink this fine wine 'til we're mellow. If we don't get loaded, we'll get some more. I'm ready to celebrate, even if it's Monday. I'll tell you what, Mike, you can even stay at my pad if you get loaded and can't make it back home."

Beaver joined in. "If we're going to celebrate, we better find Jesse Pinetop. We can get him to bring his guitar."

"That's fine," I said, "I'm with you." I turned down Grande Vista. At Jesse's house I stopped the car and honked until that sucker came out.

He stood there looking stupid and finally he said, "Hey, Mikie, welcome home. What you guys up to? You going to lush up? Wait for me, I'll get my shoes on."

I told him to get his guitar, 'cause we wanted to sing.

"That's groovy, man, wait for me," he said.

While we waited, I turned on the radio, then told Art, who was sitting in front, to turn the dial until he got the right music. I had been busted long enough not to know what music was in. He said Lionel Hampton was on top, anything he played was groovy. He fussed with the dials and there it was, "Hamp's Boogie." We put it on real loud, so we could dig that beat.

Under cover of it all, I had some quick flashes. One day back from camp and I had taken care of very little business. For sure, I was weak. I'd only gotten as far as the corner and I'd be tore up in an hour, even before it got dark. I hadn't seen my P.O. or checked out with the school people, but—and I thought on this a while—I had met Penny. If I hadn't made the corner, this wouldn't have happened. It made by thighs warm and face flush.

"Hey, I've had my hand out long enough for you to shake. Wake up and shake it or I'll shake you."

That was Pinetop bringing me out of my reverie. I shook his hand, then he went around to Art's side. Art opened the door and he got in the back with Beaver. I put the car in gear and we moved down Grande Vista to Sixth Street, then left, and down into the gulley. Down in the gulley I turned right and drove all the way to the dead end of the block. We found a place away from the houses and prying eyes, and parked.

We were feeling pretty good by now. Pinetop took double swigs from the gallon. His explanation was that he was behind and had to catch up. He tuned his guitar and in a while he started singing softly. We tried a couple of songs, then I asked him to sing "El Corrido de Tortilla Flats." I hadn't heard it for a while. We were just buzzed enough to make it sound good.

It was getting dark by this time, so we were losing our inhibitions, or at least hiding them in the dark. Once we picked up Pinetop, we didn't look for anyone else. We would get loaded then, hit the corner or the courts and see what else we could make happen.

The singing was good, then the jokes began. Art told some about Mr. Peanut and Mrs. Nut. We cracked up on them. They probably weren't funny, but we were relaxing and getting stoned in the process.

I remember getting to Art's house. We went in and I said hello to his mother and father. I tried to carry on a conversation with them. They were very nice people and very non-judgmental, so I always tried to put up a clean front for them.

We lay in bed in Art's room, talking about the day's events. We didn't talk too long before drifting off to sleep.

Somewhere around eleven o'clock the next morning, Art's mother came in and asked if we were ready to get up. Art woke up in a bad mood and took it out on his mother. I kept my mouth shut, but it bothered me to hear him holler at her.

o   o   o

Driving home I started the usual routine. Where was I and where did I want to go? Let me see. First, get home and clean up. Second, go see that damn P.O. Third, go see the school people. "Once I get past them, what's next?" The answer to that was number four: decide on where to go looking for a job. Here I had an option. I would check out the guys to see where they were hiring, and if nothing was happening, I would tell the old man to get me a job at the restaurant where he was working. This was my last choice, 'cause I didn't want to be tied down at night.

Now that I had thought out the business end of things, what was next? That was easy: girls! Penny. I tried to push her out. It didn't work. I started playing with her in my thoughts. For one, I would go to her house and see her folks again. For another, I would treat her clean, like I would save her for when we got married. I would cut down on drinking and messing around with the guys. I would really go to school and get a job that would pay good and get my car in good shape. The folks had met Penny that Christmas and liked her, 'cause she was clean cut. They would want me to be with her again.

All this daydreaming got me as far as the house without my really seeing where I was driving. While I was busted, I had gotten curious about where I lived in L.A. I had promised myself to take a better look. Promises, promises, and I wasn't keeping any of them. Well, what could I expect, I'd only been out one day. At seventeen I had plenty of time to live and love and see and do. I figured these good days would never end. Why should they? All I had to do was play it cool and take care of my body and mind. I'd get there, wherever "there" was.

I parked the car, went inside the house and ran into my father, who hadn't gone to work yet.

"Where you been, *m'ijo*? You're only home one day and you're already worrying your mother, that's not fair."

I agreed with him that I shouldn't have stayed away. I told him that I had called home when it got late. I didn't tell him I was too drunk to drive. He asked if I had a hangover. I lied and told him no. I wasn't hung over, but my stomach felt kind of uncomfortable.

o   o   o

In the next several days, I took care of business. I went to the School Board over on Grand Avenue. They had my Metro High School transcripts, but not the credits I'd earned at Camp Malibu. This bothered me, 'cause I couldn't enroll in school until these credits were added to my transcript. That way, maybe I could get enough credits to put me in the eleventh grade. Even so, it was embarrassing to know that instead of the twelfth, I had to be placed with younger kids in the eleventh grade. Well, that's what screwing around will get you. One thing, I'd be way sharper than any of those kids. I looked young, so I would probably seem like a whiz kid.

The visit to the P.O. was a drag. That hard-nose was no Horvath. I had expected that there would be a connection between the camp and the field office, but I was wrong. This guy started off by telling me that he didn't give a damn about my record in camp. The thing that counted now was that I stay straight out on the street. He got on my case immediately.

"First off, let me say this, my name is Mr. Barber. I've got a caseload that is too large to handle, so I'll only make one home visit or two. I'll expect you in here once a month. I might get some volunteer to help with your supervision. Since you're seventeen, I don't care if you go to school or not. You pachucos don't do good in school, anyway. So, the schools would rather not have you. Now, I expect that if you don't go to school, you better get a job in a big hurry. Don't come up with no crap that you can't find a job, because they're hiring everywhere. Your probation will last for six months, then you come in. If you've done your job by following instructions, we'll cut you loose. If you haven't followed instructions, we'll continue you. Now, once again, I'm overloaded with work, so I won't screw around with you. You stay clean, and I'll take care of you. If you don't, I'll simply send your ass back for more training. If you're thinking of joining the service, I can work with you on that. Looking at your jacket and looking at you, it's obvious you're a pachuco. That don't cut no ice with me, as long as you follow the rules and don't try to play me like you was a tough guy. Here's some forms to fill out. Mail them in and be ready to come see me whenever you get a call. I'll be by your home soon, but I won't announce it. That's all for now, so get out and get going."

All this time he had punctured the air with a long forefinger for emphasis. I got up, looked at him dead in the eyes for a few seconds, thanked him for his time and walked out without shaking his hand. He would have to figure out why. His calling me a pachuco and equating that to being a loser didn't escape me. I felt the chip on my shoulder starting to build up. What did I have for him? As far as I was concerned, he could stick it. So could his system. I wouldn't go back to his institution, but it wouldn't be because he helped keep me out.

I left the office and drove over to the neighborhood to see what was happening. As I was parking, I noticed Alicia crossing the street and going into the Barrilito. That was the name of the hangout. Alicia was with Rachel, but Penny wasn't with them. My heart did a bumpity bump and I swore. I went into the Barrilito. The girls saw me and said, "Hi," in a real friendly way and meant it. That was the way it was with Alicia, though. In a way, I was always sorry that she saw me only as a friend and that was the extent of her interest, because she was really fine. On the other hand, if I couldn't make out with her, it was great to have her for a friend.

We picked a table and sat down. Rachel was friendly, so I didn't snipe at her. They asked what I'd been doing. I gave them a run down on my trip to the Board of Education and the Probation Department. I wasn't particularly proud of the latter, so I minimized it.

Alicia said, "I knew you were upset about something. Have a coke and try to cool it, baby."

I said, "Life on the outs is great. I want to continue being a part of it. It's going to be tough, though, 'cause of all the ass I got to kiss. Aw shit, let it slide."

I changed the subject by asking what was new in school. They talked about their classes, about noon time and the football rallies and stuff like that. They capped it by telling me that Roosevelt was playing Jefferson Friday night and asked me if I would like to go. If I did, they could buy me a student ticket and I could go with them.

"Yeah, I like the idea. Are you going with any guys or are you telling me I'll be going with you two?"

"Uh huh, us girls and you," Alicia said. I was cool as I told them we had a date. Maybe I would ask one of the other guys to come along. If not, it would be my pleasure to escort two girls. My, but things were looking up. I reckoned I'd bust my cookies behind all of this.

∘ ∘ ∘

On Friday I picked up Art. I had asked him to come with me to the game. He readily agreed when I told him we would be going with some chicks. This didn't get him excited. He was quiet but also very good looking and never had any problem making out. He wasn't girl hungry. It was nice to escort girls to the ball game, but the ball game was the big thing to him.

We decided to make both the "B" and Varsity games. The "B" game started at six o'clock, so we picked up the girls at five thirty at Alicia's house, then made it over to Roosevelt just about the time the kick off took place. We gave our tickets to some guy in an ROTC uniform who eyeballed me and Art. He couldn't place us, and he was trying to play the part of being a hard-case. I started to stiffen, but Art told him to be cool. Meanwhile, the girls turned on the charm and we cleared the ROTC.

After we sat down, Alicia said, "Say, Mike, you sure aren't as loose as you used to be. You get mad in a hurry now. Take it easy."

I told her, "Play dead. I don't like no fool trying to play it cute with me. That ROTC guy was just trying to show off because of you two."

Art cracked up on me. "Take it easy, tiger, you'll live longer."

Rachel said, "Well, Mike was right, that fool didn't have to act bad like that." I thanked her.

By the end of the evening, the "B" team had lost and the Varsity had won. As the gun exploded, signaling the end of the game, we got up and headed for the exits. I noticed that Alicia was now with Art, while I was with Rachel. Rachel was being a hell of a good date. We walked slowly through the crowd and out to Mott Street where I had parked the car. Alicia got in the back, followed by Art. I opened the door on the passenger side and let Rachel in, then went around to the driver side and got in. I looked at Rachel a long time. She looked good to me. I wanted some action and figured Rachel would be game.

We drove off. I made a tentative move with my arm, checking to see if Rachel would move over next to me. She did and I felt cool.

"All right back there, where do we go from here? Are you game for some booze? What kind do you want?"

The girls said they would go for some sweet wine and that it would be fine to drive to the beach.

I asked, "Say Rachel, what time do you have to be home?"

"Oh," she said, "this is my night out, so I can be out until two o'clock. But what I can do is call home and get an okay to stay out later or tell them I'm staying with Alicia."

"What about you Alicia?" I asked over my shoulder.

"What are you worrying about me for Mike?" she shot back kind of laughing. "I'm a big girl now. You don't have to protect me."

"Sorry, baby," I said, "I guess you're right. I keep thinking of you as a kid and you're right, I want to protect you. Shine it on, okay?"

We parked in front of Frank's Liquor Store. Art and I got out. We pooled our resources. It was easy with him, because he liked to pay his own way. Don Juanito, a local drunk, passed by. We greeted him, then asked him to do us the favor of buying some wine for us. He was glad to accommodate us for a taste for himself.

Having found that we had plenty of time to be with these girls, we decided to drive to the beach. Instead of going down Pico to Santa Monica, we decided to go down Sunset Boulevard. Now, that was a real ride. It seemed like we drove all night and would never get there.

Once we passed UCLA, I started looking for a place to park. This urge came about because I had been looking in the rearview mirror and saw that my two friends were past talking and now were doing some passionate necking. I guess Rachel had also picked up and she too was pressing in on me. I had been talking on and off with her while listening to music on the radio. I was trying to figure her out. Was she really game or was she just a lot of talk? Should I try to score, when I hadn't even really kissed her? Man, I was really getting ahead of myself, or was I? As I talked, first to her, then to myself, I started to sweat and kind of get the butterflies.

"Hey Art, should I park for a while?" I hoped he would say yes.

"You better not, the cops patrol here and we're not from

around here and we have booze in the car. I bet that as quick as we stop, we'll end up being their guest in the can." Damn, he was right. I'd have to wait until I got to the beach to start my campaign.

Rachel seemed to sense my feeling of despair. She got up real close and kissed my cheek. "You're all right," she murmured. "We'll be together when we get to the beach."

I liked that. I turned and smiled broadly at her. "How about a drink from our Tawny Port, baby?" She unscrewed the cap and gave me the bottle to drink from. It was chilled and felt good going down. I handed her the bottle. She took a good swig and capped the bottle. I wondered if she was getting anxious along with me. I hoped she was.

On Pacific Coast Highway I turned the car south and drove until we found an open parking lot. I drove in, paid the quarter for parking and drove down the parking lot away from other cars. I parked, sighed and asked for the bottle of wine again. This would give me time. Either Rachel or I would make the first move when I put the bottle down and capped it. She asked for the bottle, took a swallow and capped it. I moved towards her. We popped our teeth against each other in our effort to get it going. I could feel a taste of blood. I didn't know whether it was my blood or hers. Frankly, I didn't care.

We were going pretty strong within a short time. While coming up for air, I looked towards the back seat. My friends were watching us. It embarrassed the hell out of me. I really never had cared to have anyone watch me. I asked Rachel if she wanted to walk on the beach. She said yes, so I opened the trunk of the car and pulled out a blanket. We didn't say anything to our friends. We just took off, me with my blanket and she with our bottle of wine. We walked on the beach, getting sand in our shoes and looking for a private place to put down our blanket. We finally found a place we liked. I shook out the blanket and we sat down on it. We talked quietly about nothing. I drank again and handed her the bottle. She killed what was left of it. We had done in a quart of wine and I figured now it would do us in, but what a wonderful way to go.

We were well loaded. We sat up and I held her in my arms while we listened to the crash of the ocean surf on the shore.

We were sitting like this when Art and Alicia stumbled into us.

"How's things going man?" Art asked.

I said things were going fine. "We've been sipping our wine, having a good time and talking. How 'bout you two?"

Alicia had her arm around Art's waist. She was acting like she controlled him. Like she was announcing that he belonged to her.

Rachel and I got up and walked along with them for a while. I started staggering a bit too much, so I suggested getting back to the car. When we got to the car I crawled in the back. Rachel was cool, she got in the back too. We smooched until I got bored. Art and Alicia got to the car.

I told Art, "You drive 'cause I'm going to relax in the back."

"Yeah, man," he said, "I've been wanting to drive your wheels for a long time, anyway." By the time he drove out of the parking lot I was asleep.

The next thing I knew, we had crossed the bridge to the city across the river. Rachel was snoozing comfortably next to me. I massaged her breasts, kissed her cheek and woke her up. I wanted her wide awake by the time we dropped her off, so she wouldn't catch any heat from her people. I kissed her warmly, then let her out of the car. She said I didn't have to walk her to the door, so I didn't.

I lay back in the seat as Art drove off to leave Alicia. She said, "Remember my party tomorrow. Be there or be square."

Art parked the car and walked her to the door, where they kissed and said a few things to each other. I let Art drive to his home.

We talked about our good times.

Art said, "Mikey, I'm hooked on Alicia. It's nice but it's a bummer too, 'cause I want to stay single and play the field. I don't want to go steady, but I don't want to lose this chick."

For my part, "I like Rachel, but nothing moves inside my gut for her. It was nice being with her, but I haven't been home long enough to know what I want. I'm gonna see her at the party and take her out. Maybe we'll spark later on."

We changed the subject, going on to other things. For the first time, I talked to someone about my camp adventures. I told him that I had learned a lot about getting along with people. I really didn't want to do anything bad, but if the barrio was fighting, I'd continue getting involved.

"Man," he said, "if you got that attitude, you might as well join David in the service. I got my notice and I'm glad I'm leaving. I don't like anyone spitting on my corner, but I need a rest."

I left him off, then made my way over to Alameda and on to the pad. I wasn't high by then, so I drove carefully, knowing what I was doing all the way home.

The music on the radio was mellow. Slow and quiet. I thought of life in camp and life on the outs to date. I chewed on what Art had said. He surprised me. I figured he'd walk alone soon.

How about Penny? Damn, I didn't even want to think of that square chick. Just to prove to myself that there was nothing happening, I tried to conjure up a picture of her. What did she look like? What was her shape like? I was right, I couldn't focus in on her.

Chapter XX

I visited P.O. Barber and told him I was in school, but still needed a job. I also told him that I didn't want to work in a restaurant and they probably wouldn't hire me at Lockheed, since I had left them kind of suddenly.

"Look here, Mike, I've been reading your jacket. Mr. Horvath really wrote a case view on you. Guys like Mr. Fisher from schools and even the F.O.'s and the O.D.'s got in the act on your behalf. The way they wrote you up, you were too good to be true. So I got your school transcripts, beginning with grammar school. I've decided that you are a damn fool. You got everything going for you, including people who believe in you, yet you're screwing around in that barrio with that pack of losers, digging a deeper hole for yourself.

"This is what you're going to do. You're going to go to the Swanson Steamship Line in San Pedro, get a ship and ship out in whatever job they got available. I'm going to set up an appointment for you. You keep it, or your ass is going to be mine. One thing for sure, I'm spending too much time with you and your chicken-shit existence and it's pissing me off."

The more he talked, the angrier he seemed to get. I guess I had gotten to him. Maybe he wasn't used to extending himself. He contained himself long enough to give me the name and address of this fellow at the Swanson Steamship Line. He wrote a note of introduction and told me to take some small snapshots to be used on a passport and Coast Guard identification papers.

For my part, I said, "Thanks a lot for going out of your way, sir. Sorry I upset you. If you call Horvath and the rest of the camp, give them my regards. You're right, I've been goofing off. I guess I can live without the barrio and the boys, and I don't want to take another fall. I'll let you know how I make out." I got up and walked out. He didn't offer his hand and I didn't offer mine.

Once outside the building, I evaluated what had taken place. The sucker had gone out of his way for me. He was telling me that my salvation was in getting out of the clutches of my barrio. He was afraid, and probably right, in figuring that I would do a repeat performance in some institution if I didn't split. He didn't ask me if there was any action in the barrio, so I didn't tell him. But yes, there was action and yes I had been involved. Penny had been working on my mind. Yes, I'd finally decided to check back in with her.

I shook her loose from my thoughts for now. I wanted to concentrate on this gig that would take me away from it all. How crazy. This might be fun and it was considered patriotic to be in the Merchant Marines. They had been getting plenty of press lately because so many were torpedoed. There I went again, fantasizing, wanting to be a hero, a respected hero, a Chicano hero. I wanted to be someone Penny could be proud of. That last thought snuck in there unannounced.

At the corner, I ran into Beaver. I told him about my conversation with my P.O. and his wanting me to join the Merchant Marines.

"Why don't you let me go with you. Maybe I'll get lucky and get to go too."

"All right, come along. Anyway, I can use the company. I'm kind of nervous myself."

We went and had our pictures taken, then went back to the corner.

"Surprise, Momma, I'm home and I'm staying in tonight. I got a job offer and I'm going to get up at five in the morning, any questions?"

I shot all this at her at once, then left the room. She just looked and smiled 'cause I was loose. I made a few phone calls, kind of lying around on the couch and talking trash to the chicks.

I called and talked to Penny. By the time I hung up, I had made a date for the next night to take her to the show. I felt real good after talking to her. Thinking about the guys at the corner, I would probably get some razzing if I was seen with Penny again. But all of a sudden I didn't give a damn and

I would defend my position. I figured that I would even tell
Angel where to put it, if he didn't like my going out with her.
"Oh, oh," I thought, "I wonder where I'm going with this. I
could fall for her again."

The next morning I picked up Beaver and took off down
Figueroa Avenue on a one way street to San Pedro and our
future.

At the Navy yard there was a check point with Navy Shore
Patrol in charge. I told the dude that I had an appointment to
see a Mr. May about signing on with the Merchant Marines.
He said okay and gave us directions. I thanked him, intending
to be very civil today. I really was intrigued with the idea of
shipping out and so was Beaver.

We found the Swanson Steamship Lines' office, parked the
car and went on in. We went over to a desk where this nervous
type guy was sitting. We told him who we were and why we
were there. He looked up with a sour look on his face. He told
us to go across the street to another building and sit there and
wait until he was ready for us. Beaver looked at me and said,
"Be cool, my man." I told him I would and for him to be cool
too. We went across the street and sat on a bench outside the
building.

There were some guys standing around talking Spanish.
Not Chicano Spanish. I wondered where they were from. I
didn't ask them. After a while, this guy who said his name
was Mr. May came out from his building and walked across to
where we were. He looked at the Spanish-speaking fellows and
said, "All right you assholes, get over to that building. Keep
your mouth shut and don't give me none of your shit. You
fucken greasers give me a pain in the ass." I couldn't figure
out what the hell he was all heated up about. It bothered me
that those dudes didn't talk back. They just hung their heads.

I stood up and asked those guys where they were from.
They said Nicaragua. I asked them if that country grew balls
on their men. They said yes. "Well then, why are you taking
this asshole's shit?" I asked.

They didn't answer. Instead, May came up and chested
me. "What the hell are you mixing into this for? You keep to
yourself and mind your own business or else!"

I blew my cookie. I asked him, "What the hell do you

mean 'or else?'" "You think you're bad enough to kick my ass? You're nothing but a chicken-shit Paddy that don't have no balls. You push people around who don't know how to defend themselves."

I stuck my fist in his chest. It made him grunt and spit his cigarette out. With no one around to back his play, he ran back across the street. I followed after him calling him names. He made it to his desk, pulled a drawer open and came up with a gun, which he pointed in my direction. That brought me up short, but didn't cool me off. I still moved in his direction.

We must have been loud 'cause the Shore Patrol showed up. May screamed at them to get me out of there. They told me to get my car and drive out. One of them got in with me. I told Beaver to stay behind. "That asshole may make a connection between the two of us." I was escorted to the gate. The guy with me got out of the car and told me, "Keep on going and don't come back."

As far as I was concerned, they could shove the whole outfit. I was hot and stayed hot all the way home. Dammit, I had gone there with the best of intentions. Knowing that the barrio had its grip on me for sure, that even if I went out with good girls, I could stay clean for only a few hours. If there was a beef, I was expected to be involved and I would be involved. Sometimes I might even start the beef myself. I got home, parked the car and went inside the house.

My mother asked how it had gone. "Did you get the job, m'ijo?"

"No, I didn't. They tried to get smart with me and I got mad at them."

"Ay, my son," she said, "you ought to watch that temper. Well, come and eat some frijolitos and rice. You'll feel better after you eat."

I was still steaming over my latest put-down. I shrugged it off after a while and sat down and ate. Afterwards I went out and worked on the car. I cleaned the insides, then wiped the paint down. I didn't have the energy to wash it, even though I had this movie date with Penny and I wanted to impress her. "I did?" By golly I did want to impress her. One thing, thinking about her got my mind off my stinking day.

Beaver showed up towards the late afternoon. He said,

"Man am I tired. By the way, that son of a bitch May really acted tough after you left. He couldn't handle you there, but when you left he kept telling all of us what he would have done if the Shore Patrol hadn't taken you away. He called you a chicken-shit Mexican pachuco and all kinds of other names. I passed their examinations and got hired. I'll be getting my papers from the Coast Guard, then I'll ship out."

"That's all right, brother," I said. "I mean about getting the job. As to that jerk and what he said, I would sure like to test his ass outside that ship yard. I'd bet he'd piss in his pants. I'd even give him the edge with the gun. Maybe I could have one too and we could have a shoot out." I sounded weird.

Beaver didn't say anything. He started to laugh, I guess to ease his tension. We went inside the house and asked my Mom to feed him. We talked about his upcoming adventure and about my having to face my P.O. before the week was out.

"Man, that P.O. is going to burn your ass. What you gonna tell him?"

"What can I say? I'm going to tell him the truth, but before I do that, I'm going to check out a couple of leads for jobs. That way when I walk in, I'll be enrolled in school part time and have a job. That'll soften it for me. The thing is that he wants to save me from messing up again, and he figured that if he could get my ass out of the barrio, I might have a chance. I was all for it, but you know I've only been out of camp a few weeks and I think I have a lot of making up for time lost. I want to mess around, go to parties, check into things. Maybe I'm all mixed up. I want to do all kinds of things, but I don't want to go to jail anymore. Well, you got me saying more than I wanted to. When I was in camp this was called counselling. You blew it out and your counselor listened and made suggestions.

Beaver was cool. He wasn't interested in going to jail. He was always game for a fight, but he rarely pulled anything stupid, other than getting drunk too often. That was nothing I frowned on 'cause I did the same thing.

"Look Beaver," I said, "I have this show date with Penny so I'll give you a ride home, then I'm going over by the neighborhood to pick her up. If you don't want to go home, I'll drop you off on the corner."

He smiled at me, with a big, broad grin. This meant he was going to come on strong about something. "I heard you were taking out Angel's sister. She's not your type. How come you're messing around with her?" he asked.

"I was kind of making it with her before I got busted. I don't want to get serious again, but I enjoy her company. I've seen her at the maltshop and talked to her there. I decided on a change of pace, so I'm taking her to the show, maybe to the Meralta or the Vern."

He said, "You see, man, you're starting to get stuck. If you weren't interested in that *muchacha*, you would take her to the Crystal or the Joy Theater," and he laughed.

I knew that it was teasing on his part, but he was getting my goat, 'cause I hadn't been able to sift out in my mind what it was about this chick. She was different. She was different 'cause she didn't seem to care that she walked alone, meaning that she didn't need a crowd to make it. She sure didn't put on any fronts. Her conversation wasn't really that interesting either, unless she got on school subjects and the future. That's when I tried to impress her and didn't know why. Man, I'm saying she was mixed up and it was really me.

On our way to T-Flats we crossed Alameda and turned right on Macy past the railroad station. There was plenty of activity there. All kinds of servicemen getting leaves and arriving in L.A. Some were going home on furlough after bootcamp, maybe for the last time. Some were coming in from overseas. You could tell the ones that had been somewhere 'cause they had ribbons on their chests. They kind of strutted and swaggered when they walked. They were heroes. They had a right to strut. I wondered if any had been here during the Zoot Suit Riots that sent me away.

I turned left on First Street and headed across the river to that other city that belonged to the *raza*. "Yeah, it belonged to the *raza* and it was going to stay that way. If they didn't want us anywhere else, then we would stay here and do our own thing." Now what the hell was burning me?

When I got to Fresno Street I let Beaver off, then turned right to Gleason, then down the block to Penny's house. It was the same white house, well kept up, with a lawn and flower pots by the porch. It still had that white picket fence around it and a gate to go through. I went through the gate and up to the porch and knocked on the door. Penny opened the screen door and I stood there waiting to be asked in.

She simply said, "Hi."

I said, Hi, and asked, "Can I see your mother to get her okay. to take you to the show?"

"Come on in and I'll call her," she said. No smile, no excitement, just kind of matter of fact.

Her mother came into the front room from the kitchen, wiping her hands. "Good evening ma'am. Remember me? With your permission, I'm taking Penny to the show. Probably to the Vern Theater. We'll be back as soon as it's over, 'cause I know it's a school day tomorrow."

"Yes, I remember you. Where have you been? Never mind. Be careful and keep your promise to have her home early." And she shooed us out the door.

We turned and walked towards the car. I felt pleased with myself, because I behaved in a nice way and was able to talk with some class to Penny's mother. I had put on some squares and my hair, which had grown out, wasn't combed as wildly in a ducktail as it could have been.

They had two movies and a cartoon, which we sat through. One of them was a war movie which was called "Thirty Seconds Over Tokyo." This movie had to do with the early bombing of Tokyo by a squadron of American planes. It was inspiring. Everybody in the show cheered for the Red, White and Blue. I remember reading about the incident in the paper while I was still busted. President Roosevelt had been asked where the planes came from. He had been quoted as saying, "They came from Shangri-La." This wasn't too clear to me at the time, but everybody else seemed to get a kick out of the comment, so it must have been witty.

Driving home, we made small talk about the movie, about school, about dating. When we got to dating, she told me that this was her first time out with a boy since I had gone off to camp.

As we talked, I reached for her hand. She kind of kept it in, not extending it to me. I told her with some tenderness, "I'm reaching for you, please trust me and reach for me too. It'll be okay. I want us to be friends again. I want you to trust me. I like you. I want you to like me again."

Now she turned her head and looked at me fully, and for a long time. Finally she said, "I want us to be friends. I want to trust you. I want to like you, I want you to like me again."

She made my heart thump all over my chest. This girl was a total experience. I got her home, stopped the car and started to get out and open the door for her.

"Do you want to kiss me?" she asked.

Here I was, trying to act cool, and she came on again.

I said, "Yes."

She came to me. We kissed but it was still awkward.

"Look Penny, don't worry about it." She said, "I'm sorry I'm so bad at it, but I haven't kissed a boy since you left."

"Well, as far as I'm concerned, that's all right with me."

A couple more get-togethers and I took her to the door. I thanked her for the date and told her I'd call her again.

Chapter XXI

I got up next morning feeling good. I ate, gave Pablo a ride to school and then I drove down to the Frank Wiggens Trade School. I figured on taking Body and Fender Work, then when I learned something, I would move over and study auto mechanics. I could also take a few formal school classes that would give me some high school credits. I was facing myself. "What the hell are you going to do for a living in the future? You better get hip to yourself." I needed something I could make a living from and at the same time keep me out of the bucket. A high school diploma was nice to have, but it wouldn't put beans and tortillas on the table. My old man was right, get a job that'll bring money into the home. "Paddy's get education, Chicanos get jobs," said that wise old man.

I had no trouble enrolling at Frank Wiggens. They asked me for three dollars to process my paperwork. I paid that and told them they could get my school transcripts by calling up the Board of Education. They phoned while I was there. The transcripts were now available and in order, including the credits I had earned while at Campo Tres. I was through by noon. They told me to come in the next day, sign in to Body and Fender and American History. I would be there four hours a day. That meant I could get a full-time job or a part-time job. Well, that would be the next stop.

Before I left, I put a call in to my P.O. He was out to lunch. I asked if he had any other appointments for after one o'clock. They said no, so I decided to suck it in and go get it over with. By the time I had driven across town to East Los Angeles, it was after one o'clock. Mr. Barber was there waiting for a report on my job interview at the Swanson Steamship Lines.

He didn't take my part at all. "You acted like you did when you first got to camp, like an idiot. Who the hell do you think you are? Can't you get it through your head that I'm trying to do the right thing by you?"

I started to get hot after a while. I looked everywhere but at him. If I focused on him, I was going to try to jam him and there would go our rapport.

When he finally ran out of breath and assorted swear words, he asked me, "You have any plans of your own?"

"Yeah, I got up this morning and enrolled at Frank Wiggens. I'm taking up Body and Fender Work and American History this semester. That's four hours a day. That'll leave me plenty of time to find either a full-time or a part-time job. I have job possibilities at the restaurant where my father works and at a factory where this friend of mine works. He said they would hire me. They make life boats. It's kind of a metal shop." As an afterthought, I told him I had this square chick and would be taking her out regularly. This would keep me from being around the corner so much. He nodded in seeming approval.

What I told him took the wind out of his sails. He looked at me for a long while, tapping his pencil on his desk during this time. I got the feeling I had blown his mind. I'm sure that he felt that after I had blown the steamship company gig, he should write me off his books as a lost case, and now he wasn't so sure about me.

I got up to leave and he told me to let him know where I decided to work. I told him okay, and as a parting shot I told him that, no matter what the consequence, I was a Chicano and a man. I couldn't bow my head and let anyone shit on me. I hoped that some day he could understand that. He pursed his lips but didn't say anything.

Chapter XXII

It was Sunday morning and I was sitting around nursing a hang-over from the night before. The phone rang, jangling my nerves. I answered, saying "hello" in a flat voice.

"Hi, it's me. I wonder if you could come over today and see me?"

I almost choked. I forgot my dry mouth and huge head. It was Penny.

"Yeah, I can come over. What time would you like to get together?"

She told me it was twelve o'clock and she knew I lived kind of far away, so one thirty would be okay with her, if it was okay with me.

By one thirty I was parked in front of her house. She came out of the house, walked down to the car and climbed in. She closed the door behind her and sat there for a minute. "Hi," she said once again.

I said, "Hi." In a way I was mimicking her.

"Could we go for a ride, maybe out to the country?" She asked the question in a tentative manner, not really used to asking or giving directions. I thought of Crystal Lake, which is off in the San Gabriel Canyon area just past Azusa. I had been there a few times on picnics and parties in the past.

It was a nice day for a ride in the country, even though it was kind of cool. After all, it was now late in November. We drove down Valley Boulevard after leaving East Los Angeles, all the way to Azusa Avenue. From there we turned north towards the hills.

We small-talked about school, about the movie we'd seen the other night, things at home, things at the corner and so on. A couple of times I stopped off on the side of the road to admire the view and do a little light-weight hugging and kissing. She asked questions about the neighborhood and I went into a detailed account of what life in the barrio was about. Towards the end of my account, I looked over at her. She seemed to be listening, but not really hearing. I decided not to go on too much about T-Flats. I probably had turned her off.

"Why don't you find a place to park where we can be by ourselves?" she asked.

This knocked me over, but I did as I was directed. I drove slowly until I found a place where we could park off the road. She moved over to me, held my head in her two hands, looked at me with that smile of hers and said quite simply, "I love you and I want to make love with you."

I sat there dumbfounded. I had let her get under my skin. I had been in love before, but never like this. I couldn't figure her out before, and I couldn't figure her out now. What should I do? I wanted her. I was aching for her, but I didn't want to violate her. We made out, that's as far as I let myself go.

Driving back, I held her close to me. I drove very slowly, 'cause the road did a lot of winding and was narrow. This was okay, we weren't in a hurry to get anywhere. I felt nothing but tenderness for her. I smiled at her. She asked me to stop the car so she could kiss me. We kissed several times, then we took off down the hill again. We finally got on Valley Boulevard and headed east towards our barrio.

"Penny," I asked, "how do you feel right now about us, what we did and about our future?"

"To tell the truth Mike, I'm scared. But we're together and things are going to be all right. As for the future, things are going to happen between us and I'll be happy. If things are not meant to be, I'll be sorry, because I do love you."

For my part, I started thinking of the future. That future included Penny. I sang to her. It was a song that Billy Eckstein sang. It wasn't real popular, but it had been David's favorite song. "Somehow I know that you're the one I care for, the thought of you just lingers on a while. Somehow I can't forget you, you're everywhere, you haunt my every moment. At times I know I must have been unfair to act as though I really didn't care, but now I'm so sorry I treated you this way." There was more to the song, but this best fitted us and our mood.

I wondered what David would have said or thought if he had been with us today. David had stayed on my mind. I felt it appropriate that he be with us now. God, I wished he was here. We'd plan a wedding and he would be best man and Martha would be the matron of honor. I'd have to write him right away about all these happenings.

Penny looked at me and said, "I think you're sensitive about people and their feelings. You really aren't like anyone I know. By the way, I love the way you sing and the songs you pick to sing."

Before getting out of the car, we kissed and she said in a very quiet way, which of course I had found was her way, "You are precious to me." She left me blushing and feeling like a kid and I had no comeback.

○　　○　　○

I got the job at that factory. They made lifeboats on contracts with the Navy. They gave me a chance and I did all kinds of things, like driving the tow motor, spray-painting with zinc chromate, riveting and things like that. The pay wasn't spectacular. It wasn't even a dollar an hour, but I worked steady and got in some overtime in order to make a few more dollars. If I assessed what I had going at this time, I was way ahead.

Things were nice at the pad, except for Pablo, who continued wanting to be busted. At least, he seemed to want that. P.O. Barber was happy with my progress. I was going to school regularly. I enjoyed the Body and Fender class. The other classes were helping towards a high school diploma. I was going out with the *batos* to parties because that had to be. I was staying away from trouble, even though I was hearing some word about my not being available and maybe I was turning into a rat. That hurt, and soon I would have to face up to it.

The reason for the shift in priorities was Penny. I knew it and she knew it, but the barrio being what it was, I could share it. Well, in a way I could. Penny and I did a lot of double-dating with Art and Alicia. Since they were pretty well hooked on each other, they recognized the same in us. It was two couples going to shows, dinner, some dances in out-of-the-way places and long cruises. We necked a lot, talked some and respected each other's privacy while enjoying each other's company as a foursome. Strange, we never talked of moteling or even sex during these times. We talked about getting married and doing everything right.

Chapter XXIII

A year had gone by and it seemed long, because so much had happened to me.

During the Christmas holidays I was invited to Penny's home for dinner. Angel was home on furlough. He was surprised when he opened the door and saw me standing there. I guess nobody had told him I was coming to dinner.

"Hey man, how did you know I was home? I can't make the corner yet. I'm having dinner with the family. I'll see you at the corner later. I'll tell you all about it."

Penny came up behind him. "Mike didn't come just for you, Angel. He came 'cause Mama and Papa invited him for dinner and because we've been going out together lately."

Angel looked at his little sister and then at me. I looked back at him and he seemed to be getting bigger and badder. "Wow, we're going to have a session here in a minute," I thought.

He smiled and asked if I knew the rest of the family.

I told him that I did.

"What you been up to lately, man?" he asked. I skipped the time in camp and told him I was going to school and working. In between I thought, "Ain't this something, getting interviewed by one of the *batos* from the corner as to what my credentials were. Was I good enough to be in his damn house with his damn family?" Of course, all the time I acted cool and was at my most charming best with all of the relatives and only held hands with Penny in a loose way. I found myself sucking up to Angel, not liking it and not doing anything about it. At the very least I could have walked out and made it to the corner, but I didn't.

I hung in there through dinner. Then towards ten o'clock, Angel said to me in a rather meaningful way, "Let's hit the corner and see what's happening. I want to see if there's any action." I agreed that hitting the corner was a good idea. I thanked Penny and her parents for a fine evening. I made it a point to tell Penny, in front of Angel, "I'll call you tomorrow."

∘   ∘   ∘

"Hey, Butcher, Eddie, how crazy, both you guys on furlough at the same time with me," Angel greeted those two.

I fell out myself because these guys were real buddies. We hugged each other, then looked around to see who else was there. We were standing outside the Malt Shop, which was closed. Art showed up with Johnny, saying they had the night off from their girls. They said Beaver was home too. He had gone off for a while, but that he would be back real soon.

"Say," I said, "why don't we try to get into Evelyn's Cafe? All you guys are in uniform and looking like heroes. Maybe they'll let us in."

They agreed, so we walked down the block and went on in. I was right, Evelyn let all of us in. We toasted each other and told stories about what we had been up to. Butcher, who was in the Navy, seemed to have gotten the worst of it. This was more evident the drunker he got. He talked about the shooting and strafing and killing and ships going down and people screaming. I was glad I hadn't been anywhere near where he had been.

Beaver walked in and we hollered over to him and greeted him noisily. He was wearing a Merchant Marine uniform. He smiled all over the place. We ordered a beer for him. We put two tables together, because there were about ten of us, and told Evelyn to keep the quarts of beer coming until closing time. She smiled a lot and accommodated us. I wondered if Evelyn was catering to us 'cause business was bad that night. Maybe it was because she was being patriotic and the guys were in uniform. For sure, she knew we were not of age. Well, if she treated us straight, we would behave the same way. We took over the juke box, playing everything they had in it from Chicano music to boogie and even one or two cowboy records. The rest of the customers got a free ride. They were older men from around the neighborhood. They had their sons in the service, so they approved of "our men in uniform" drinking in the same place with them.

The conversation switched to girls. This gave everyone a chance to trot out their favorite stories about scoring. The guys who were in the service talked about the trail of broken hearts. Those of us who were still here talked about the over-abundance of girls. The chicks would go out with you, even if you were younger, because there wasn't that much action left around.

"What about you, Mike?" Angel asked kind of innocent like. "What have you been scoring with lately?"

I froze up. "I've slowed down to a walk, Angel, 'cause I'm going kind of steady, as a matter of fact, with your sister Penny."

"Yeah, well I wanted to talk to you about it," he said.

I looked around at the guys. They were busy bullshitting one another and weren't paying any attention to us.

He got up off his chair and kind of looked at me. No malice, no nothing. I had no desire to get hit while sitting down. I got up and I got knocked down. I got up and Angel was walking towards the bathroom. The guys stopped talking and looked at me and at Angel's receding back. I got up and walked towards the head too. Butcher asked if there was going to be any blows. I said no, that Angel was just making a point. The guys settled down.

In the head, Angel was relieving himself. I did the same. He finished, then talked as he washed his hands. We had been drinking a lot, but he still came across real sober. I watched his face as he talked.

"Look man, when I left home I told my folks not to let my sister mess around with any of the *batos* from the barrio or any other barrio. It's because we're losers. We won't give any girl a chance to be good. Look at the way we talk when we're together. Nothing but making out and screwing. Running girls down. Well, I want to save my sister all this. She's got a better chance if she makes it with some guy who doesn't belong in a gang and who goes to school. A square is what I want for my sister. I like you. I've always liked you, but you're like me, too game to do crazy things. If you mess around with my sister, I'm afraid you'll drag her down."

I started to defend myself and my feeling about Penny. I told him, "Just 'cause your mind is always on your pecker and you don't care about anyone except yourself, don't mean everybody is like you." I told him I didn't appreciate the punch on the mouth, but I could understand what he was saying and feeling, 'cause I had a sister too and I had told her to stay away from the *batos*. Funny, all of sudden I agreed with what he was putting down.

"You know, Mike, you go ahead and go with Penny, but do me a favor, take care of her, 'cause she's had problems growing up. I punched you in the mouth to get across the idea that I don't take her lightly. Don't let me hear you talking about her."

I retorted, "Penny is my business and only my business. I don't advertise. I don't know about your upbringing, but I was brought up to respect women. I don't let nobody spit on my corner and the same goes for my girl. I have Penny nearly on a pedestal. She's still in high school and she shares her dreams of the future with me, like going to college and stuff like that. She makes me feel good, that's why I try to stay clean. Have you heard me talk in a chicken-shit way tonight about anyone or anything. Yeah, maybe she's had trouble growing up, but that's okay, 'cause we can handle it. One other thing, you got your point across, but don't try to hit me again, 'cause it'll take more than one punch next time!"

Angel stared at me for a while, then stuck out his hand. "Good luck with my sister, man, you're going to need it, 'cause you've only seen her sweet side. From now on, whatever happens, you earned it." We grinned at each other and walked out of the head. I felt good. I mean, real good. Good God, it was good to be here with these fine *batos*. I wondered where we would take it from there that night?

Beaver said, "Let's go to Shep's Playhouse."

I asked, "What's that?"

"It's an after hours joint over in Little Tokyo. I heard it rocks and stays open all night long. They have Joe Liggens and his Honey Drippers there."

"What's the deal with after hours places?" Art asked.

"Well, we have to pay a dollar each, then we bring in our own bottle and they sell us 'set ups.' A 'set up' is a bottle of soda with glasses and ice for our group," explained Beaver.

Johnny started making the collection. You could depend on him to do this. He managed to keep a couple of bucks for himself that way. We collected enough for four fifths of whiskey. Johnny stashed two bottles in my car and two of them in Butcher's car. That would keep us going after we left Evelyn's at two o'clock in the morning, which was closing time.

By two o'clock in the morning, we did in all the beer on the tables, and since we had someplace else to go, we didn't cause any trouble about leaving. For sure everyone was lushed up. I wondered who would be in shape to make it to the next stop. We had grown to twelve guys and no girls. We were noisy and happy and drunk. In the next couple of days it would be Christmas, but for us it was Christmas tonight, and would extend for all those days and maybe into New Years. For my part, I was flying high.

Of the twelve of us who started for Shep's Playhouse, seven of us made it up the steps and were sober enough to appreciate Joe Liggens as he and his group played all that fine jazz. I was stiff as I sipped my drink and listened to the music. At six o'clock in the morning they swept us out. We must have been good for the business. They asked us to come back and we promised we would.

I don't know who drove my car. We ended up in Butcher's driveway. Since I was kind of awake, his mother asked me to come in. I looked at the guys asleep or passed out and figured they wouldn't miss me. I made it to a couch in the front room and knocked out. I remember feeling good.

Chapter XXIV

That holiday season was the greatest. A lot of the guys came home on furlough. They weren't kids anymore. They were a lot more serious. They were scared. They drank heavily. They tried to screw everything in front of them. They wanted to fight. They were angry at us for not being old enough or stupid enough to join up. They were mad because they had seen friends get killed and couldn't figure out the logic of it all. Some of them were coming home on furlough and bringing their friends with them. It was funny how many of them had made friends with Paddies. We took those Paddies in, showed them a good time. We dressed them up in drapes and let them go out with our girls and taste our home cooking. If one of our *batos* had told his Paddy friend that we were the greatest barrio and people in the world, we went all out to make the story true. We also scared the piss out of them with our vicious gang action. It was funny because they had seen all kinds of bullets flying, but this barrio violence was so personal that, battle scarred as they might be, this shit still scared them.

Since Angel had given us his blessing, Penny and I had been at ease with each other and the rest of the world.

My mother was still happily impressed with Penny and my father had patted her on her bottom, which pissed me off. I didn't want anyone touching her. I didn't want my father acting like we were a couple of kids.

Pablo had been wheeling and dealing grass. He had gotten a lot of it spread in different barrios. Now some guy from State didn't want to pay him what he owed. Pablo asked me to go with him to collect. Much against my better judgment, I said I would. We made it over to State. As it was, we'd never been friendly with them, and now Pablo was going into business and spreading out, whether these barrios were friendly or not.

In a way, it wasn't so bad, 'cause it wouldn't be like messing up someone from a friendly barrio.

We had decided that Pablo would ask this guy "Jap" for the money. If the guy shined him on, I would come on with him. I had a gun with me that I had borrowed from Art. I figured I would pull it out if things got hot or if we had to convince this sucker that he should quit and pay off.

I wondered why I was backing Pablo's play, when I hated the whole dope business. I guess it was because he was by brother, because he had asked for help and because, if I needed help, he would be right there without questioning the why of it.

When we caught up with "Jap," he was standing on the sidewalk outside a house. We parked the car and got out. I stayed by the car while Pablo went over to talk to him. Jap acted too cool. He either had a lot of help in the house or else he was carrying a piece and figured to get it out quickly, if he had to. He told Pablo he didn't have the bread for the *mota* Pablo had given him on consignment. If he wanted, Pablo could wait a few days and he would have it. I called Pablo back to the car. "You stay in the car. If I start pushing this jerk around, start the motor and open the door on my side. This guy is trying to get away with something. We may not get your money, but we better screw him up or we're going to get a bad reputation."

Now, I wasn't thinking about anything except that punk looking at us. He didn't seem scared. He didn't try to split. It was like he figured he had everything wired in his behalf.

I walked over to him. "Say, cool, do you know who I am?" I asked.

"No man, I don't know you," he said.

I told him, "I'm Little Mike from T-Flats. I want you to know, 'cause if we don't get straight today, I don't want you telling any of your guys that some *batos* came here and messed over you without telling you who they were and where they were from and especially why you got beat on."

I pulled my gun out and spat, "Come up with the bread you owe the man." I thought he was going to shit.

"I swear I don't have the money. I made a bad deal and didn't collect the money."

I let him squirm before telling him I believed him.

"Why didn't you say so to begin with, asshole?"

I hit him on the mouth with my left, then I hit him in the stomach with my right. When he came forward, I checked his pockets. He had a nice looking 25 automatic. I took it from him. The door to the house opened and a couple of guys came out. I recognized them as they walked towards me in a menacing way.

I told them, "Let it lie. This beef is small, but it can get big if you make me pick my gun up and point it at you. If that happens, we'll have a real beef. We just want to straighten things out with Jap. You guys know these deals have to be cleared up." They agreed and backed off.

I went back to Jap. "Look here, mother, this thing isn't over. Pablo is going to stay on you. If you don't get straight with him, I'll get into the act. If you're going to be a big time dope dealer, you better know how to be honest or you won't live to be eighteen. I chested him, then turned him loose.

He agreed, "I'll do right, man, I promise."

On the way back to T-Flats I told Pablo that his beef was not over. He might as well look over his shoulder from now on. I figured the same for me. This kid Jap didn't scare that easy and the *batos* from State didn't like the *batos* from T-Flats for a lot of reasons. He assured me that he would stay alert, that if there was a beef, he would be in the middle of it, even if he had to get hurt.

The beef with the guys from State came off, but Pablo was not involved. Pablo was busted along with a couple of other homeys on robbery charges. His beef was big enough so that by the time he had gone to court and they had done him in, he was on his way to Preston School of Industry, which is an institution in the California Youth Authority. The way I saw it, Pablo had been waiting for a long time for this bust. He finally got his wish. I felt sorry for my mother and father. They would have to go through the whole affair with him that they had with me. That was a bummer. They had to spend money on a lawyer for him, because the D.A. wanted him tried as an adult. In the in-between, Pablo found out that cops have big feet and they know how to use them. He found out what it's like to get the shit kicked out of him. This had a lasting effect on him. He never again was a great supporter of law enforcement agencies.

Chapter XXV

Winter passed and spring came. Penny, Alicia and Rachel graduated along with a few hundred other people. I went to the graduation exercises. I played the adult part, but secretly, I felt jealous of all the "kids" who were getting their diplomas. I really liked the procession and the music they played.

By this time, everyone knew that Penny and I were going steady and I was completely hooked. That was okay with me and my family and Penny's family too, but a lot of times it wasn't okay with the *batos*, because the barrio was losing its grip on me. There was plenty of fighting and I was constantly involved in it, but it seemed the barrio was never satisfied. I kept going to school, but not with too much enthusiasm, and I kept working, but again with not too much enthusiasm.

The only thing that gave me any stability was the P.O. who didn't let up on me. No matter how well I did, he still stayed on my case. I wondered why and he told me.

"Look, pachuco, as long as you're wearing that uniform, no matter what good you do for yourself on the one hand, you undo it all on the other hand by refusing to give up on the barrio. On occasion I get sheriff's reports on the action on the streets. Your gang has come up a few times and your name too. You're still on their roster. The day they're able to make you for anything, they'll bust you, and I'll probably go along with them, because I'll know that you've been putting me on all along."

He was right, even if I didn't tell him so. One other thing that came to mind which helped stabilize me was my fear of getting busted again. It wasn't that I wouldn't pull easy time. The joints were full of people who knew me. I had a good rep and that would hold me in good standing. What I didn't want was to make time by the numbers. I just didn't have that kind of time to give away. I left the P.O.'s office feeling low. I knew damn well that whatever I wanted counted for nothing, 'cause I honestly couldn't handle my action.

As I did so often when I was feeling low, I picked up Penny and went for a cruise. After a while I stopped the car, turned her around to face me and asked her, "Would you leave with me if I asked you to go?"

She said she would.

I asked her if she was curious as to where we were going.

She said, "I'll go with you anywhere, anytime."

I said, "We'll leave Friday night for Yuma. You tell your folks and I'll tell mine. I'll get a hold of Art and Alicia, maybe they'll come along for the ride."

She said she would be ready on Friday for the big trip. I started the car up and drove over to Hollenbeck Park. We parked and walked around. I noticed people looking at us. I wondered what was wrong. It finally hit me that I was all draped out and the squares didn't seem to go for it. I looked at Penny to see if she was getting any reaction. She seemed oblivious to it as we walked along holding hands.

"You know, Penny, about that trip on Friday. Maybe we better forget it. What I'm asking you to do is probably to throw your dreams away. As a matter of fact, I'm sure you've figured out by now that your brother was right. You hook yourself up with a barrio bum like me and you've bought trouble for yourself. You know that when I'm with you I'm straight, but when I leave you and go with the guys, I'm way different. That difference is hurting you right now with your folks and it'll probably hurt you later on, because I won't be good to you. I love you, but I'll end up screwing things up, because I'll still be hanging around that corner."

She searched my face for a long time. There was no emotion. Her eyes were flat, no sparkle. It seemed like she too was hurting. A few hours ago, she had gotten a proposal of marriage; now that proposal was being rescinded.

She finally spoke. "You know that trip on Friday? Well, I think you meant we were going for more than a ride. I figured by the time we got back we would be married. I want that. I have only a piece of you now, but if we get married, I'll have all of you. You don't know how much I want that. I don't want to share you with anyone and I only want you. I'll be a wife to you and I know you'll grow up and you'll be somebody, too. I know it. It's funny how I'm the one who has the reputation of moping around, but you do a lot of it and it hurts you. It doesn't help. Quit being so hard on yourself."

She brought me out of my downer. By the time I took her home, we were both high on each other again. I promised myself again I wouldn't touch her until after we were married. Married? God Almighty, I hoped I was doing the right thing. I knew I had the right girl and I finally had figured out that, if I wanted stability, it would come from being responsible for somebody other than myself.

∘ ∘ ∘

By Monday morning when I went to work, I was a different person. Mr. Married Man got up, cleaned up, had breakfast prepared by Mrs. Married Woman. It was hard leaving that morning, 'cause one goodbye kiss led to another, and I was beginning to ease my way back into the house. Stability, responsibility and all that other stuff took hold. A gentle push in the direction of the car and I was gone. For sure, I'd be back that night, though. Wow, I'm married. I wondered where it was going to lead me? I thought about this over and over, but it was pleasant wonderment. It wasn't hard to swallow at all.

On the way to work I tried to put things in their proper perspective. I finally gave up. I really couldn't think that clearly. For one, I would ease the word out among the guys at work that I was married. Maybe after lunch I would go into the office and ask the boss for a raise. I would tell him I needed the extra money because of my new obligation. I hoped he'd see me as an adult with responsibilities. I thought about the guys again. They would crack jokes and make crude remarks. I would have to go along with them for a while, but then hold the line so they wouldn't get the impression that they could be vulgar about Penny and me.

The marriage and suddenness of it all took our two families by surprise. But we got past them without any objections. I got a lecture on what being a married man was all about, first from my parents and then from Penny's parents. Penny's parents wanted assurances that I would take good care of their daughter.

Penny's father said, "It's true that we didn't want her getting involved with anyone from the corner. That's why Angel told Penny not to date you or anyone else. You boys are too wild. We were worried when she started dating you. You're young, you're wild, but you're a good boy, and my wife and I believe you'll be good for Penny. We're counting on that."

I thanked them for their confidence in me and assured them I would live up to their expectations. I meant it too.

The days passed for Mr. and Mrs. Married Couple. We were happy. I concerned myself with making Penny happy. She concerned herself with making me feel like a man. There was some dependence, but mostly an interdependence. We knew that if we took care of each other, there was nothing else we would need.

Towards the end of the week, I finished work, then went to see the P.O. I was feeling good. No pain at all. I was married, hadn't been to the corner in a week, had gotten a raise and wasn't doing too bad in school. I had a full schedule and frequently got tired, but it was a good tired.

I went in smiling and shaking his hand. He wanted to know what that was all about. I let it all hang out. He tripped me up. Didn't I know that I was a minor? Didn't I know that I was on probation, and had to get permission from him and the court to get married? Didn't I know that he could revoke my probation and send me off for something called statutory rape? So it went with him.

Damn, I could never win the Mr. Sunshine award in his eyes. I didn't know how to act with him. If I kissed up to him and told him I was sorry, he wouldn't go for it. If I got pissed off, we would probably meet in court. It was best to cool it, let him work it out and give me the result of his decisions.

He read me off for my stupidity. I let him blow, even though being called stupid really got to me. One day, when I was off probation, I was going to challenge this jerk, just to see if he was tough when he didn't have a hold on some poor slob. I held my mug.

When he got through, I asked him, "How about you making a home visit? You can take a look at how we live and you can talk to Penny. If we look good, you can decide in our favor. If we look bad, you can jam me. Let me remind you that I am eighteen and soon I'll be off probation and your caseload. If you jam me, you'll only have to work overtime on my case."

He shot back, "Screw you, pachuco. Don't tell me how to do my job or give me any of your smart mouth. I'll be over to see you next Monday night after you get off work. You better look good. Now get out of here."

I left, once again not shaking his hand or saying goodbye. In a way this guy was starting to remind me of Horvath. Both of them wanted to be nice, but they were overworked and probably used to getting jived by more than half their caseload. I wondered what it would be like to be a P.O. I figured it would be cool, and I would be a good one.

I got home feeling a bit down. Penny understood my feelings, but was glad I had stayed cool and had invited the P.O. over to look us over. We were living in a three room-apartment over in City Terrace. We had been lucky to get this place. It belonged to a friend of my father's. They lived above us. They were nice pleasant people without being nosy. Mr. Garcia said he felt sorry for me getting married so young. "You haven't even reached your prime and you're already fried," he used to say. His wife would tell him to shut up and mind his own business. They had gotten married before his prime too. He said he regretted it, but he didn't seem to mind it too much. He would crack up and say that I at least had a way out. If life got too dull or was a drag, I could always join the service. He wasn't far from wrong. I wouldn't be joining the service, but I had turned eighteen and was eligible to be drafted. Of course, I had to be off probation and in no trouble with the law. I wondered if Penny would be very upset if I got drafted. I really couldn't bear the thought of splitting on her. Not now, not when we were doing so well.

We had a good night that night. There were rockets exploding. The lovemaking was good, clean and honest. We were learning to share one another.

o　　o　　o

A lot of guys just can't stand prosperity. I guess I was that kind of guy. The P.O. had come and checked us out. As I figured, Penny had won him over. We had no trouble as far as the courts were concerned. He suggested that I might get an early release from probation. The job was all right. I had a raise coming. School was fun again and I probably would be getting enough credits to be in the twelfth grade soon. Everybody liked me and I liked everybody. I had even gotten a chance to visit Horvath to show off Penny and my new attitude toward life. He was impressed.

One Friday night after supper, I got an itch to make the scene at the corner, just to see what was up. I would have a few beers, bullshit with the guys and then be home by midnight at the latest. Penny didn't put up an argument, which was cool. She understood that a man had to have some free time every now and then. That a woman knew how to treat a guy so he could feel like a man. I really felt good about that. I kissed her long and hard before I left. I promised myself to make extra good love to her when I got home.

Chapter XXVI

At the corner some of the guys saw me as I drove up. They came over to the car and started their teasing. "Hey, Mike, what happened? Ever since you got married, you don't even come out of your bedroom. What do you do in there? Is it true that you've joined the *batos* from City Terrace? How come you're favoring us with your company tonight?" I let them ride me. Their good natured bring-downs were pointed. I hadn't made the scene since I had gotten married, except to drive by on my way to Penny's folks' home.

"Look, fools, when you get married, you're supposed to play the part. Who the hell is supposed to take care of your old lady? I'm here, though, ain't I? Now, what I want to know is who is going to start the collection, 'cause I'm thirsty and I got the night off."

Ganso, who I hadn't seen for a while, was down visiting from the hills of Geraghty. He came by while I was talking. He put his hand out for me to shake.

"Congratulations on your marriage. Welcome to the club. But what a fool. You don't have to get married to get it."

"Yeah, well, if you don't have to, then why did you get married, Ganso?" One of the onlookers said.

Ganso answered, "You know what, for a guy whose never been anywhere and isn't going anywhere, you sure come on strong. Let me give you a hug, then I'm gonna knock you on your ass."

The kid backed off. He couldn't be sure whether Ganso was serious or not.

Ganso pulled a couple of bucks from his pocket. I reached into my pocket and pulled out two dollars to match his.

Art said, "Beer is fine, but let's get some wine. Wine is fine in the summer time, but even better in the spring time."

J.C. asked him if he had been practicing to have a show down with Chato on who could come up with the best poetry.

"You try to talk like a poet, but you're no poet and your feet show it."

By this time everyone was cracking up. We were all in a good mood. We sent Art and Eddie to Clover Territory to pick up some jugs of wine. The rest of us made it over to Henry's house by the Fourth Street bridge. We stopped at Frank's for some quarts of beer.

At Henry's house we opened a quart of beer for each of us. There were ten of us in the house and it looked like before the night was over, the number would double. Henry's two sisters where there. They put on some 78's and the guys danced and flirted with them. Johnny brought out some dice and we shot craps for a while. It was smoky and noisy and a lot of fun for me. I had forgotten what a kick being with the *batos* from T-Flats could be. I sat back for a while and checked it all out. Marriage was fine. I really dug it, but there was another need that had to be filled: the camaraderie that could be found only at times like this.

We were somewhat loaded by the time Art and Eddie came back. They didn't have any wine and they obviously had been in a fight. Art was swearing and acting wild. Eddie was calmer, but he too was agitated.

"What happened to you *batos*?" I asked and started getting heated at the same time.

Eddie answered, "We made it over to that place by Clover. The man said he didn't have any wine, but gave us an address to go to over by State. We stopped at this address he gave us. There were some *batos* standing on the corner. They were loaded, so when we passed by them, they asked who we were, where we were from and what we were doing in their barrio. I told them what was happening, but they got bad. Before we punched out, Art and I tried to tell them that T-Flats didn't have any beef with State. We were cool with them. They laughed and said we didn't have our balls. Art blew it and hit some bastard, then they jumped us. Art went crazy, but they still messed us up."

Art hollered, "All right, so we didn't have a beef with State before, but we do now. Those bums dared us to come back.

Are we going back?"

I was all worked up. I was high and I hadn't gotten in a beef in a long time. I remembered the last time Pablo and I had been to State. I was heading out the door and hollering at Art and Eddie to come with me. The rest of the gang came out after us. Henry pulled his Chevy out behind mine. There were twelve of us. Six in each car.

Generally I kept a cool head. This time I was worked up. Nobody was going to mess over our guys or bring down our barrio. Not while I was around.

I jammed the brakes on as we hit the corner of State and Brooklyn Avenue. There were about six guys standing there. Art and Eddie flew out and ran at them screaming and punching. Henry and his boys got out and within a few seconds all hell broke loose. There I was, swinging and hitting. I got hit a few times, but it only made me madder. We kept hollering out who we were and where we were from. They kept wanting to talk. They finally ran and we chased them for a couple of blocks.

I came out of my trance, stopped and headed back for the car. "Let's make it," I kept hollering at the guys. We were finally loaded up. I had the car rolling as the last guy piled in. I took off watching to make sure Henry didn't have any trouble getting started up. Now that I was out of my trance, I was thinking that with all the noise we made, there would be reinforcements and cops in a short while.

When we got back to the neighborhood, we decided to park the cars in the courts and sit around in Henry's garage. We figured that if the *batos* from State Street decided to pull a raid, they wouldn't hit Henry's house.

Everybody felt good about the raid we had pulled. Art and Eddie had been backed up. There hadn't been too much action lately, so they needed the exercise. We had gone on an adventure together and this drew us closer.

"Hey, Eddie, where's the wine we sent you for?" Ganso honked. We had forgotten about that.

Eddie told us to jam it.

"Well, then, what about our collection?"

Eddie told Johnny he hadn't chipped in, so not to be asking about it.

Everybody laughed, "what a cut-low."

There was no booze and it was too late to get any, so I decided to head for my pad. I said good night, promising to come back to the corner more often. None of the group knew Penny too well. I wanted to bring her over to meet them. I wouldn't stand for them saying anything bad about her, but I didn't want to fight them all. The only way was to get them to know her. "Once they know her, they'll back us, because she's so great," I thought.

○ ○ ○

I went in the house, made it to the head, cleaned up, washing the blood off me. Some of the blood was mine from a cut lip and a bloody nose and some belonged to somebody else. Whoever that was, he was hurting some place, all because he couldn't be friendly to strangers. I kind of cracked up at that.

After I cleaned up, I went to the refrigerator. There was a quart of beer there. I opened it, then went to the bedroom. I turned on the light on the nightstand, then took off my clothes and lay in bed, drinking my beer and looking at Penny's sleeping face. After a while she stirred, then woke up. She propped herself up. After I had kissed her, I gave her a rundown on what happened. Like a big fool, I bragged about what I had done. You know, I acted like I was a soldier doing my duty. Taking care of my own, protecting our people from the enemy. I really got caught up in it. She listened attentively, sometimes smiling, sometimes frowning. What a woman. She never criticized my actions. She never got excited about it either.

After I finished drinking my beer, I got up, went to the head and relieved myself. I put on my pajamas, turned out the lights and moved in close to Penny. She seemed to hold me extra tight. After a while, we made love. She really worked hard at it, almost desperately. This was not too surprising to me, because while she was generally slow and easy about most things, when it came to us, she really got wound up. Maybe this is what got to me about her. She was so private about her feelings when it came to me. She never disapproved of what I said or did. She let me be me. No reproach for my actions.

○ ○ ○

A few days later I was at work when I got a call to come into the office. I figured that I was about to get that raise I'd been promised. I walked into that office smiling and I walked out the front door between two cops with my hands cuffed.

One of the cops said, "You're wanted for questioning for attempted murder. Come with us."

My jaw almost fell out of my face.

On the way to Hollenbeck Station, the cops asked me several questions like, "Where you from, what you been doing evenings?" They said, "We already have some of the guys busted. They fingered you as the guy who used a hammer on some guy's head in State. That's how we knew about you."

I told them, "I don't know what you're talking about." I knew they were bluffing. No matter what they might know about the beef at State, for sure I didn't use a hammer on anybody's head, and for sure none of the *batos* copped out to anything.

I got fingerprinted, then placed in a cell. I began to get down. Not because of what I had done, but what it was going to mean to Penny. I didn't want to be busted for such a chicken-shit beef, but I could handle it. I got to wondering who fingered the barrio and who had the hammer. There was nothing to do now but let the play go on. I figured that in good time, things would work themselves out. No use worrying too much, since all I had used was my fists. I knew I wasn't going to volunteer any information to anyone. Not now, not later. I took a nap.

o   o   o

The P.O. had been his usual pissed-off self, but he also had been cool with me. Mr. Barber let me out of jail while I waited for court. The problem now was whether they would try me for assault as an adult or as a juvenile. To me the whole deal smelled. They had taken me and a couple of the guys, Henry and Art, to juvenile court. They had accused us of a lot of things and then boiled it down to assault, even though they had no witnesses. Henry and I were on probation, so they had a hold on us, regardless.

The good citizens were still upset with the violence of the "damn pachucos." That was us. Someone had to go. That was us. On the other hand, we kept hearing or reading where the good people kept saying that "If those goddamn Pachucos want to fight, they should join the Army."

My P.O. argued in my favor. We ended up in juvenile court where he told the court that I had been a model citizen since getting out of camp nearly a year ago. He told the court, and I agreed, that if given the chance, I would join the service. My records from camp were also looked at. The judge agreed that I would probably make a good soldier. I might not have had any desire to be a soldier before going to court, but I sure did as I stood there talking to the judge. I wasn't going to go back to camp or to Preston, even if I felt I was being railroaded.

Henry didn't do as well. They felt that he needed some camp time to rehabilitate him. Art, they felt, was Army material. Joe, one of his brothers, was in the service already and his other brother was missing in action. This would leave his mother alone. His P.O. figured that, one way or another, his mother would be alone and at least this time it would be an honorable absence from home. As far as I was concerned, Art got a good break. I should talk, though, setting myself up to judge anybody was the last thing I should be doing. Art and I would probably be shipped out together pretty soon on the so called "buddy system."

Penny had not gone to court with me. She preferred to stay at home. She hadn't said too much about the total affair. I hadn't been able to figure her out. I imagined that she was deeply hurt for me. I played the martyred part. Boy, was I stupid. I needed a lot of growing up. "You don't stop playing the fool," but I didn't say that to myself until much later. That happened when I walked into the house and found Penny gone. She had left me a note. She was going to stay with her mother until she could sort out our relationship. She told me that she felt like a traitor deserting me when I needed her, but it seemed to her that I wanted the corner and what went with it more than a home with her, that it must have been a drag having no excitement. She understood, but she didn't know how to cope with it.

Later on in the day, she called and asked to meet with me. On the phone she sounded like a person who had made up her mind about something. We met at Hollenbeck Park. We sat on a bench watching the cars pass by. The people stared out at us, we stared back. People walked by. They looked at us. We looked at them. She talked. I forced myself to listen, not talk.

"I've been thinking back on the last year. I don't think I could have made it without you. As a matter of fact, I know I couldn't. I'm strong enough now not to have to lean on you, depend on you. I love you now, but if I continue with you, I'm afraid I'll grow to hate you. I don't want it to come to that. We can remain friends. It should be enough for the both of us. There should be nothing more."

I concentrated on what she was saying, picking out key words, like love, friendship, thank you, dependency, hate.

She waited for an answer. I stared straight ahead, searching within me for the right words. The right phrases. All the while I was holding her hand. We were sitting close together. I reached out and stroked her hair. I leaned over and kissed her cheek.

Finally I said, "I've been preparing for this all day. Yeah, we'll stay friends, but a divorce is a divorce. You're setting me free and at the same time you're asking for freedom for yourself. As for your dependence on me, well that goes both ways. While I've been supporting you in your needs, you've given me something. You've given me an outlet for my feelings and thoughts which, as you know, I hadn't been capable of expressing before. While I know I've helped you, you've helped me too. You've satisfied a yearning in me. You've filled a gap, an unexplainable gap. I thank you for that."

She laid her head on my shoulder, no, closer to my chest. My heart beat a little faster. She cried softly. I kissed her forehead, then looked up again, noticing the cars passing by.

"What's happening?" I asked myself despairingly. She began talking again.

"Lately, I've been thinking about our future. It's a dead end. We aren't going anyplace together. I want to be able to see a beginning with someone and a visible end. With you there is only the past, the here and now and no future that includes me. That's wrong."

She stopped talking. She looked out at the cars passing by, absently rubbing the fingers on my left hand. She did this as a matter of habit. I smiled ruefully. Here was my cue to show my bruised ego. She had unloaded me. She did it gently. There was no mention of my going off to the service. God only knew what might happen to me in basic training and afterward. Combat in some country away from her. Was this anyway to treat a martyr?

I got ready to tell her where she could stick her friendship and love. But I held back. She was right. She was a human being with the right to her decisions. She was making one now.

I turned, faced her and said, "Please listen to what I say very carefully. If you cut me loose, I won't come back to you. I'm going to have it rough enough adjusting to Army life, without having to worry about you, but I can do it with or without you."

This was the first time I'd ever talked nasty to her, but I had to take the crud I had in me out on someone and she was handy. She rolled out a few tears, but said nothing.

For my part, the words kept coming. "Maybe I'm playing the macho part ... "

She nodded as she looked into my eyes. At the same time I didn't want her to say she was wrong out of a feeling of pity. I wasn't going to put my head down and pull a hang-dog expression, even if I felt like it.

I searched her eyes, but saw nothing out of the ordinary. I saw no relief there that she had been able to say the words that would set her free from me. Indeed, while we had gone through all this talk for the past hour, I still saw the same expression there I'd seen in the past. Love and trust. There was nothing indicating relief.

She finally said, "If I get involved in anything, it is going to be making sure my life from now on is run by me and for me. I'm going to get involved with myself. I'm going to join the living in the same way that you have joined the Army. I've decided that I love you, but I also love me and that it's about time. It will be serious time. I'm going to work at it. Will you help me?"

I nodded. I knew I would. We kissed warmly and walked back to the car holding hands. She went back to her family and I went back to those *batos locos* from T-Flats until I reported to Fort MacArthur for some Army time and a change of uniform.

This is how it ended between Penny and me. But not between my barrio and me, because I came back to it and I'm still with it.